BROTHER PHILIP

SECRET OF THE ANDES

Illustrated by David Singer

LEAVES OF BRASS PRESS

Secret of the Andes
was first published in 1961 by
Neville Spearman, Ltd, London.
First American edition
published in 1976 by
Leaves of Grass Press, California.

ISBN: 0-915070-02-2 (paperback)

Design: Jon Goodchild
Calligraphy: Mark Twain Behrens

FIFTH PRINTING 1998

CONTENTS

The ORIGIN of the BROTHERHOOD of the SEVEN RAYS

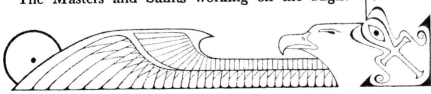

LEMURIA IS THE NAME for the last part of the great Pacific continent of Mu. The actual destruction of Mu and its submergence began before 30,000 B.C. This action continued for many thousands of years until the final portion of old Mu known as Lemuria was also submerged in a series of new disasters that were terminated between 10,000 and 12,000 B.C. This occurred just prior to the destruction of Poseidonis, the last remnant of the Atlantic continent, Atlantis. Lord Aramu-Muru (God Meru) was one of the great Lemurian sages and the Keeper of the Scrolls during the last days of doomed Mu.

It was well known to the Masters of Lemuria that a final catastrophe would cause gigantic tidal waves to take the last of their land down into the angry sea and oblivion. Those working on the Left Hand Path continued diabolic experiments and heeded not 'the handwriting on the wall,' just as today, on Earth, millions of inhabitants are continuing to 'eat, drink, and be merry,' even though the signs of the times are clearly discerned by the true people of the Infinite Father.

The Masters and Saints working on the Right

Hand Path began to collect the precious records and documents from the libraries of Lemuria. Each Master was chosen by the Council of the Great White Hierarchy to go to a different section of the world, where, in safety, he could set up a School of the Ancient and Arcane Wisdom. This was to preserve the scientific and spiritual knowledge of the past. At first, for many thousands of years, these schools were to remain a mystery to the inhabitants of the world; their teachings and meetings were to be secret. Hence, they are called even today Mystery Schools or the Shan-Gri-Las of Earth.

Lord Muru, as one of the teachers of Lemuria, was delegated by the Hierarchy to take the sacred scrolls in his possession along with the enormous Golden Disc of the Sun to the mountainous area of a newly formed lake in what is now South America. Here he would guard and sustain the focus of the illumination flame. The Disc of the Sun was kept in the great Temple of Divine Light in Lemuria and was not merely an object of ritual and adoration, nor did it serve that single purpose later when it was used by the High Priests of the Sun amongst the Incas of Peru. Aramu-Muru journeyed to the new land in one of the silver needle airships of the time.

While the final portions of the former continent were breaking up in the Pacific Ocean, terrible catastrophe was taking place all over the Earth. The Andean Range of mountains was born at this time, and disfigured the west coast of South America. The ancient city of Tiahuanaco (Bolivia) was at that time a great seaport and a Lemurian Empire colonial city of magnificence and importance to the Motherland. During the ensuing cataclysms it was raised from sea level and a mild, tropical climate to high on a barren, wind-swept plain and a frigid arctic-like climate. Before this took place, there had been no Lake Titicaca, which is now the highest navigable lake in the world, over twelve thousand feet above sea level.

So, it was to a newly-formed lake that Lord Muru arrived from sunken Lemuria. Here, now known as Lago Titicaca, the Monastery of the Brotherhood of the Seven Rays came into being, organized and perpetuated by Aramu-Muru. This Monastery, which was to be the home of the Brotherhood throughout all ages on Earth, was placed in an immense valley that had been created during the days of the birth of the Andes, and was a strange child of Nature in that its exact disposition and altitude gave it a warm, semi-tropical climate where fruits and nuts could grow to phenomenal size. Here, on top of ruins that had once been at sea level, like the City of Tiahuanaco, Lord Muru had the Monastery constructed of gigantic blocks of stone cut only by the energy of primary light force. This cyclopean structure is the same today as it was then, and continues to be a repository of Lemurian science, culture, and arcane knowledge.

The other Masters of Lemuria, the Lost Continent, journeyed to other parts of the world and also set up Mystery Schools, so that mankind would have throughout all time on Earth the secret knowledge hidden away, not lost, but hidden, until the children of Earth had spiritually progressed to study again and to use the Divine Truths.

The secret science of Adoma, Atlantis, and other highly advanced world civilizations is to be found today in the libraries of these schools, for these civilizations also sent out wise men to found Inner Retreats and Sanctuaries throughout the world. Such Retreats were under the direct guidance and guardianship of the Great White Brotherhood, the Hierarchy of

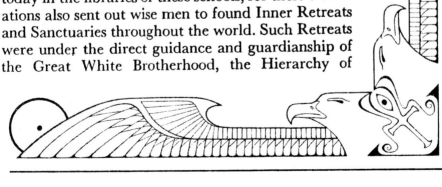

Earth's spiritual mentors.

The valley of the Monastery of the Brotherhood of the Seven Rays is known as the Valley of the Blue Moon and is located high in the Andes Mountains on the northern, Peruvian side of Lake Titicaca. Lord Muru did not immediately set up the Monastery on his arrival at Lake Titicaca, but he wandered for many years, studying and fasting in the wilderness, where he was joined by others who had escaped the catastrophes. He was originally accompanied by his feminine aspect, Arama-Mara (Goddess Meru), when he departed from Lemuria in the needle-like airship. These were not space craft, but were used by the Motherland for trade between the colonies.

The Brotherhood of the Seven Rays had known existence countless ages before during the time of the Elder Race upon the Earth about one billion years ago. However, it had never before had a monastery where students of life, highly advanced on the Great Path of Initiation, could come together in spiritual harmony to blend the flow of their life streams. Each student came into existence on one of the Seven Great Rays of Life, as we all do, and these Rays were to be blended by each student weaving his, or her, Ray, as if it were a coloured thread, into the tapestry which symbolized the Spiritual Life of the Monastery. Therefore, it was called the Brotherhood of the *Seven Rays*, also known as the Brotherhood of Illumination.

The Golden Sun Disc of Mu

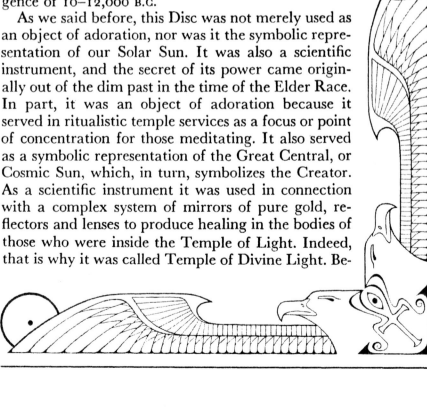

HELD BY ROPES of pure gold in a shrine in the greàtest Temple of Divine Light of the Motherland of Mu was the gigantic Golden Disc of the Sun. Before it, on an altar, which was a pillar carved out of solid stone, there blazed the eternal white Light of the crystalline Maxin Flame, the Divine Limitless Light of Creation. About 30,000 B.C. the Maxin Light went out on the Altar because of the evil of some of the priest-scientists of Great Mu. The Sun Disc remained in its shrine, however, until the time of the final destruction and submergence of 10–12,000 B.C.

As we said before, this Disc was not merely used as an object of adoration, nor was it the symbolic representation of our Solar Sun. It was also a scientific instrument, and the secret of its power came originally out of the dim past in the time of the Elder Race. In part, it was an object of adoration because it served in ritualistic temple services as a focus or point of concentration for those meditating. It also served as a symbolic representation of the Great Central, or Cosmic Sun, which, in turn, symbolizes the Creator. As a scientific instrument it was used in connection with a complex system of mirrors of pure gold, reflectors and lenses to produce healing in the bodies of those who were inside the Temple of Light. Indeed, that is why it was called Temple of Divine Light. Be-

sides all these functions, the Sun Disc was a focal point for concentration of a dimensional quality. When the Disc was struck by a priest-scientist, who understood its operation, it would set certain vibratory conditions which could even bring about great earthquakes and, if continued long enough, might bring about a change in the rotation of the Earth itself. When attuned to a person's particular frequency pattern it could transport this person wherever he wished to go merely by the mental picture he created. It was, therefore, an object of transportation.

The Golden Sun Disc of Mu was not made of ordinary gold, but was transmuted gold, and unusual in its qualities in that it was a translucent metal similar, evidently, to the 'metal you can almost look through' of the UFOs.

Lord Muru brought this Disc with him when he journeyed to Lake Titicaca, and it was placed in a subterranean temple at the Monastery of the Brotherhood of the Seven Rays. Here, it was used not only by the students of life daily, but also by the Masters and Saints from the Mystery Schools throughout the world so that they might be teleported back and forth to sit in Council or to partake of some Transmission Ceremony.

When the Incas came to Peru, and come they did, for they were not native Quechua Indians, but came from a land across the Pacific, they established a highly spiritual society on top of the ruins of the great culture that had belonged to the Colonial Empire of Lemuria. The High Priests of the Sun of Tawantinsuyo—the name of the Inca Empire—built their Coricancha or Temple of the Sun exactly on top of an older structure dating from very remote times. From ancient records in their homeland across the

Pacific they learned of the Golden Sun Disc of Mu and they knew it had been removed from the doomed continent and taken to a new land where Lord Muru had founded an Inner Retreat or Sanctuary.

Once in Peru, the Incan High Priests searched long for the Disc but were never able to locate it. However, when they had reached the place on the Spiritual Pathway where they could use the Disc to the benefit of all their people—the native, indigenous tribes they had amalgamated into an empire—as it had been used on Mu, then it was presented to them for their daily use in their Temple of the Sun at Cuzco.

The Inca Emperor at the time was a Divine Mystic or Saint, and he made a pilgrimage to the Monastery at Lake Titicaca, and there Aramu-Muru, as Spiritual Head or Abbot of the Brotherhood, gave the Disc to the Emperor. Several Brothers from the lake were directed to journey with him to the capital of the empire, Cuzco. Here the Disc was placed in a shrine that had been prepared for it, and it was secured with golden ropes as it had been held in ancient Lemuria. Even today, the holes through which these ropes passed can be seen at the Convent of Santo Domingo in Cuzco which is built on top of the Pre-Inca and Inca Sun Temple.

The Incas called their Temple of the Sun Coricancha which means Place of Gold or Garden of Gold. This was because of the magnificent, solid gold, life-sized figures of men, animals, plants and flowers that were placed in a real Garden of Gold adjacent to the Sun Temple. But the priest-scientists called the Temple Amarucancha. On some of the stones at Santo Domingo today you can still see carved serpents (*amarus*) and that is the reason, they say, that some knew the Temple as Amarucancha, or, Place

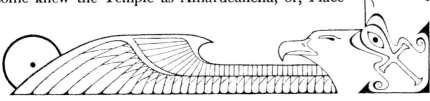

of the Serpents. However, that is not the real reason. *Amaru* is a form of *Aramu*, which is one of the names of Lord Maru. There are large snakes in the Andes which are still called *amarus*. Lord Maru's name concerns a snake because his title is similar to that of another world teacher, Quetzalcoatl, the Plumed Serpent of the Aztec Empire in Mexico. Therefore, the Temple of the Sun at Cuzco was named for Aramu-Muru, head of the Monastery at Lake Titicaca, for it was he who enabled them to have, at last, the Golden Disc in their Sun Temple. Within this greater Temple there were smaller temples or shrines dedicated to the Moon, the Twelve Planets (Stars), and to the *Seven Rays*.

The Brotherhood of the Seven Rays became the leading force in the spiritual life of the Incas, and they learned the use of the Disc from ancient records left by the wise Pre-Incas who were Lemurian colonists. The Disc remained in the Coricancha at Cuzco until word reached the priests that Don Francisco Pizarro had landed in Peru. Knowing full well what was going to take place, sorrowfully they removed the Disc from the Cuzco shrine and returned it to its place in the subterranean temple at the Monastery. The Spanish conquerors never saw it.

On January 21, 1956, Beloved Archangel Michael of the Sun gave an address at His Retreat at Banff, in the Canadian Rockies. The following is an excerpt:

Many of the Temples used on Atlantis and Lemuria have been raised into the etheric realms. Some day they will be lowered again when man is spiritually ready to receive them. It has happened that one or more of the precious stones used in the construction of these Temples have been put in the hands of a High Priest or Head of a Spiritual Order where they form a connection with the

Celestial Hierarchy. There are several dozens of the stones from My own Temple in the possession of individuals at various points on the Earth's surface today . . .

The Golden Sun Disc of Mu is one of the precious stones referred to by Lord Michael. And it was put in the hands of the Head of the Brotherhood of the Seven Rays, Aramu-Muru. The Disc will remain at Lake Titicaca until that day 'when man is spiritually ready' to receive it and to use it once again. On that day the Golden Disc will be taken out of its subterranean chamber and placed high above the Monastery of the Brotherhood. For many miles the pilgrims of the New Dawn will see it once again reflecting the glorious rays of the Sun. Coming from it will be an undeniable tone of purest harmony that will bring many followers of light up the footworn path to the ancient gate of the Brotherhood of the Seven Rays, and they shall enter the Valley of the Blue Moon for fellowship in the Father.

ᛝhe ELDER RACE

I F WE ARE REALLY to understand the meaning behind the Brotherhood of the Seven Rays and the Golden Sun Disc of Mu we must go back in time on Earth to one billion years ago.

After the Earth planet had cooled, and was ready for inhabitants, a race arrived from out of space that was not *human*, but was of the race of original *true man*. They were called *Cyclopeans*, and are known in the secret, arcane knowledge as the 'L' Race or simply, the 'Els.' Before coming to the Earth planet they traversed space following all the great cycles of Time; they were Titans who rode the starways (and they still do in another dimension of Time and Space) and sought always the best pastures of space for their flock. They were the *first life* upon the Earth and are the Immortals of our legends, the God Race or Elder Race that preceded man.

Some of the Els were true Cyclops in that they had only one great central eye in the middle of their forehead. Others had two eyes like human beings, and still others had the development of the psychic third eye. They were about twelve feet tall and were male and female, but not as we think of sex differentiation today. Before coming to Earth they had colonized much of what is known today as the Milky Way Galaxy; thousands of suns and worlds came under their influence. They usually preceded other life

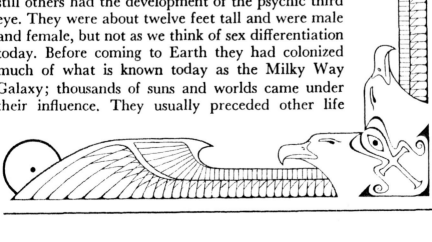

forms to a world after it was ready for habitation. Once they took up existence on a new planet they attempted to leave behind what we can only call great libraries in their deep, underground empire of enormous cities. In these libraries tiny crystal records contain the history of the Universe, and are enclosed in a magnetic field which, at times, finds an affinity with some 'sensitive' person living on the Earth today.

The Els were not exactly three-dimensional beings as we are today, although they were definitely physical creatures in a physical world. They had been attempting for countless ages, as a race, to achieve a Timeless condition, that it, to reach a place where they could not only create by mere thought, but escape from the chains of physical existence to break the ties that bound them to physical planets and systems. They were searching for the great secret that would make them Immortals, that they might march across Time and the Stars fettered by nothing.

The Earth planet was possibly the last world they colonized in the Milky Way Galaxy, for soon after their arrival here they achieved the power of creative thought. They conquered physical matter and became Gods. They annihilated Time and Space; no longer did they have need of the Earth world or the great Galaxy it belonged to. They were free! They had become true members of the Thought Universe, the Theta Universe.

Actually, the Els were not known by that name until they achieved this Theta condition. Before this they were known as the Cyclopean Race. It was their *method* of leaving physical existence and conditions that gave them the name of Els. Through the secret use of the Ninety Degree Phase Shift they abandoned the Earth and the entire Galaxy and left it vacant for humanity.

A ninety-degree angle forms the letter 'L.' There-fore, when we call them Els we are referring to a *symbol* of their race and not really to a *name*. Many words today have been derived from the name of this most ancient race. That is why they are called the *El*-der Race. The words *el*evation and *el*iminate are clearly from this source. Did not the Els *el*evate to another dimensional condition? Did they not *el*imin-ate Time and Space? If you will but look in any dictionary, you will discover some astounding things among the words that start with EL and L. Then there is the magnificent word *El*ohim; and the Twenty-Four *El*ders of Holy Scripture.

On April 24, 1955, Koot Hoomi Lal Singh (Master Kuthumi) reported:

'Over the planet stands the great Presence of the Beloved *El*ohim, *Cyclopea*. His radiation covers the entire Earth.'

Master Kuthumi is obviously referring to a mem-ber of the great Elder Race. Although, in 1956, most of the Els were no longer on Earth, they still acted as Mentors, and were usually the Teachers of the Earth's Masters or Saints. We say most of the Els were no longer on our planet, because some of them did not leave when their race achieved the Theta condition and conquered M-E-S-T (Matter-Energy-Space-Time). Because of certain karmic reactions, a few members of the Cyclopean Race did not pass through the Ninety Degree Phase Shift, and were forced to remain on Earth to work out their destiny, eventually to rejoin their race in a later age. In the meantime, they would act as Mentors to hu-man beings when the latter arrived on Earth.

Aramu-Muru (God Meru) was a member of the Cyclopean Race. He has retained the same physical form for untold ages, renewing his lifestream energy

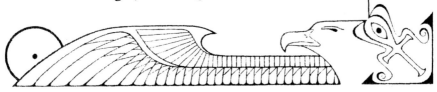

by polarization with his feminine aspect, Arama-Mara. For, as already stated, these beings do not reproduce as a hu-man does.

Lord Muru says that when he was on Lemuria he was a young student or man. However, he can mean many things by this. Perhaps he means 'young' in things Universal, and by 'man' he can mean that he is of the race of original true man. Many of the wise men of Lemuria, and earlier in Mu itself, were Cyclops. (We do not call them Els because they had not yet achieved the Theta Universe.) All of these Cyclops left Lemuria and journeyed to other parts of the world; therefore, many of the Spiritual Heads of Mystery Schools (Inner Retreats) were Cyclops who would one day rejoin their Elder Race and become true Els.*

The Brotherhood of the Seven Rays had its original beginning with the Cyclopeans since they were the first to manifest the Seven Rays of Life upon the Earth planet. These beings projected from themselves a special radiation of energy which enabled the Seven Rays of Life to be established on our planet, and without this, there could never have been a Brotherhood of the Seven Rays. Also, the Cyclopeans passed the Seventh Condition and entered Theta, the Eighth or Thought Universe.

The Golden Sun Disc of Mu was not made by the Cyclopeans, although the principle of its operation and the secret of its power was to be found in the abandoned libraries of the underground Cyclopean cities. Those sensitive enough to tune in to such knowledge in the later ages of hu-man, discovered these Truths and made the construction of the Golden Disc

*We say 'were Cyclops' because they are no longer on the Earth as we shall explain in Part VI.

possible. Thus, the Disc found its way into the life of the Motherland of Mu.

Let it be known that man on Earth will never become an L, but he will achieve a Timeless condition as they did, for the present plan of the Hierarchy is: the production of a subjective synthesis in humanity and of a telepathic interplay which will eventually annihilate time!'

While man will *not* be an L, simply because he does not belong to the Cyclopean Race (now the El Race), he will conquer M-E-S-T, and reign as a true God, a Son of the Creator.

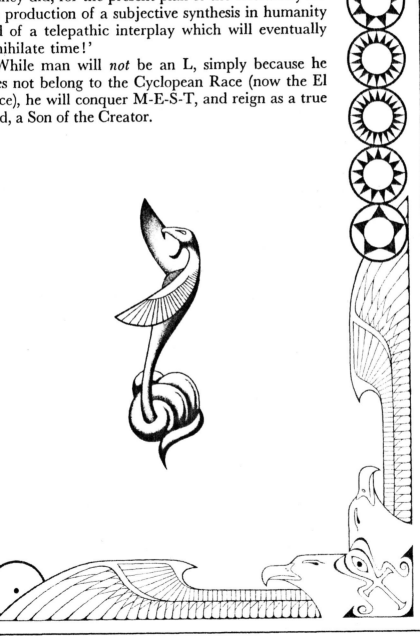

The NEW WORLD FOCUS of ILLUMINATION

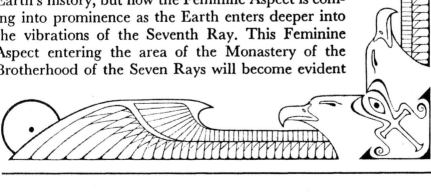

IN JULY 1957 Beloved Master El Morya said:

Those pilgrims who seek spiritual illumination and guidance from now on will be drawn to South America as they have been previously drawn into the Orient. To this end, the Directors of the Forces of Nature and the Elemental Kingdom are making preparation toward providing a natural means of access to this hitherto untapped spiritual *Focus of Illumination* in the *Andes Mountains.*

Information about Aramu-Muru's Retreat at Lake Titicaca, Peru, was given long ago to those ready for such knowledge. The *Permanent Ray* enters the planet Earth in two places. The *Masculine Aspect* enters in the Himalayas of the Orient and the *Feminine Aspect* enters at Lake Titicaca. The Masculine Aspect has been prominent throughout all the ages of Earth's history, but now the Feminine Aspect is coming into prominence as the Earth enters deeper into the vibrations of the Seventh Ray. This Feminine Aspect entering the area of the Monastery of the Brotherhood of the Seven Rays will become evident

in the future. It is interesting to note that culturally and otherwise Tibet and Peru resemble each other so much, that photographs taken of one can easily be mistaken for the other. But when we understand that these are the two areas on the surface of the Earth where the *Permanent Ray* enters, the explanation is simple.

In further confirmation of the *New World Focus of Illumination*, Phra Sumangalo, a monk at the Monastery of the Guardian Angel (Wat Doi Suthep, Xieng Mai, Thailand), recently wrote to the Abbey, saying:

'Asia is spiritually bankrupt. But you are in a region that has had its *pralaya*––rest period or spell of dormancy––and is now re-awakening to the things of the Spirit. South America is, more than any other land, the country of the future in every way, a land of spiritual promise.'

In March 1957 the Fellowship of Golden Illumination in Los Angeles, California, said:

'The call is going out continually to all on the Path of Light to *come out from them* ... the dark forces ... and unite for the establishment of the Kingdom of Love and Peace.'

In June 1952 the Bridge to Freedom activity said:

'Signs of the New Dawn! New channels are being opened, not to substitute the old ones, but to assist them; workers are coming to the front everywhere; Friends of the Great White Brotherhood are rising up from every direction. And no man can stop the on-rush of this Cosmic Christ Power releasing the Spiritual Currents of the Hour. They could not succeed, if they should be unfortunate enough to try to breast the currents of the New Dawn. Moreover, such individuals would perish under the very Law which causes the return of the generated Love they bestow, or the opposition to progress they foster. Never before as today, can it be more truly said of the Spiritual Leaders of the World, and of all the new channels, "BY THEIR FRUIT, YE SHALL KNOW THEM." '

Everywhere now, even more so than in 1952, channels of the Infinite Father's Divine Love and Wisdom are being opened and are bringing to His people words of comfort and instruction for the days of catastrophe ahead. But we are assured by the Hierarchy and visitors from space that the world is *not* going to end. Far from it! There will be many terrain changes upon the Earth, yes, but recognize these great events as the prophesied 'salvation that draweth nigh.'

For many years the Masters of other planets in our Solar System and in other Solar Systems and even other Galaxies have been in communion with the Master Adepts or Teachers resident on the planet Earth. It was finally decided in 1956 that the Mystery Schools of the Earth, operating in one spiritual body as the Great White Brotherhood, would begin immediately to disclose some of their age-old secrets and truths to the outer world!

Commenting on this decision in 1956, Aramu-Muru said at Lake Titicaca:

'... we shall not remain silent henceforward. Yet we are not opening our pathway nor our entrance to the profane, nor will the "pearls" of great wisdom be thrown before "swine," for there are "swine" upon the Earth and in the Earth. But the planet shall be cleansed of these shortly. They are not yet worthy to receive the Divine Wisdom. We are concerned with the hungry hearts and souls of thousands, and we hear their hunger and we know

within our beings that they can only be satisfied with the true manna which alone comes from our Infinite Father. Do not be surprised if you now hear coming out into the open, words from the Great White Brotherhood which is the Hierarchy for all the Earth's Brotherhoods. Now is the time for action! It is time for us to speak, and speak we shall, for we are now diligently preparing the way for His footsteps to be heard throughout the world. The Kingdom is no longer at hand, the Kingdom is *here*, and He is shortly to manifest to all men. We have awaited this time with eagerness through the long centuries. Is it not then a time for great rejoicing even though some catastrophe shall come to the world? But through this catastrophic purification man shall inherit his godhood. Look unto the "hills" for your salvation that draweth nigh. Do not despair because of catastrophe, but welcome it as the agent of Illumination and beauty. "All shall be made new" as it is written. Only the Truth shall remain!

'Henceforward, all Retreats and Sanctuaries, the Mystery Schools, the Shan-Gri-Las of the Great White Brotherhood shall work more closely together and open their doors to those ready on the Pathway of Light. Their secret hiding places will be revealed, but only to the Student of Life who stands in His Light. The Inner Retreats have been, indeed, a mystery to the outer world; they have operated in secret so that superstitious and ignorant mankind would not turn and tear them asunder. They have preserved the ancient and arcane knowledge so that the *Remnant* would inherit the Spiritual legacy in the time of the New Dawn. Now the trumpet has sounded; we hear in the distance the faint sounds of the *Seventh Trum-*

pet. The call has gone forth from the angelic hosts and we are now to make ourselves known!'

The Masters and Brothers from space will assist man on Earth *after* catastrophe, but they will not *prevent* disaster. In the post-catastrophe period they will land in great numbers, and the plan is that they will contact the Retreats of the Great White Brotherhood where the *Remnant* will be gathered together. Because of great upheavals that will take place in the Orient, Students of Life are being drawn to South America, where in the Andes Mountains the *New World Focus of Illumination* will be located. Therefore, the call continues to go out to 'come out from among them My people.' The Inner Retreats must now speak out through their many channels so that there is a *Call* for the Sheep of the Flock to hear.

The Brotherhood of the Seven Rays is working closely at the present time with the Brotherhood of Mount Shasta in California, the Brotherhood of the Royal Teton, in Western U.S.A., the Brotherhood of the Golden Robe in India, and many other Brotherhoods and Orders. Of course, there is complete cooperation with all the members of the Hierarchy of the Great White Brotherhood.

Knowledge that was formerly reserved for initiates only, now is to be given directly to individuals outside of the Inner Retreats, and men, women and children of all races will come together at these Retreats and will form a great Spiritual and Philosophical Congress. The prophesied new land will, indeed, come out of its *pralaya* and join with the Hierarchy of the Earth and the Stars to mentor the *Remnant* that will remain upon the Earth in the days ahead.

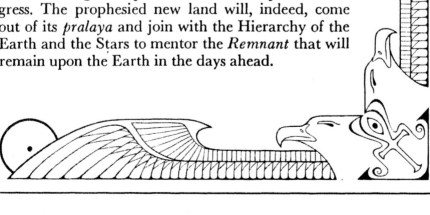

The Ancient Amethystine Order

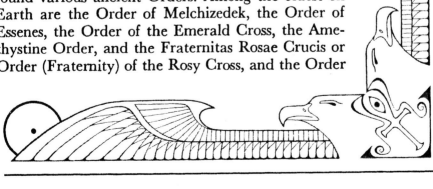

THE EARTH NOW IS entering into the vibrations of the *Seventh Great Ray*. This is the violet or amethyst (purple) Ray, whence the name, Amethystine Order.

As our world is bathed in the violet frequency, only Truth will be able to exist; all falsity will fade away of its own accord. That which has blinded man's eyes to reality will pass away before the Pure Violet Fire, like fog passes away before the dawn.

The word amethyst comes from *amethystos*, the Greek word meaning a cure or remedy for drunkenness, and indeed, is this not true? The violet or amethyst Ray will prove in its purifying aspects to be a cure for the Earth's drunkenness, a remedy for her ills. This does not mean that the Amethystine Order is going to save the world from itself, but it does mean that the Order, working in the Seventh Ray Vibration will be of great importance in the days ahead to all students of truth everywhere.

In all the Retreats throughout the world are to be found various ancient Orders. Among the oldest on Earth are the Order of Melchizedek, the Order of Essenes, the Order of the Emerald Cross, the Amethystine Order, and the Fraternitas Rosae Crucis or Order (Fraternity) of the Rosy Cross, and the Order

of the Red Hand. More recent are the Order of Mount Carmel and the Order of the Holy Grail.

All the members of the Brotherhood of the Seven Rays belong to the Amethystine Order, which is very ancient, but which assumes great importance now because its vibration is emerging on the world scene as the Seventh Ray of Life. Archangel Michael of the Sun, the Transcendent Being who is the Archangel of Protection, is the Guardian of the members of this Order, and also of the Brotherhood of the Seven Rays and all of its Outer Retreats and Sanctuaries.

Man's individuality comes under the rulership of the great Seven Rays of Life, and he is always guided by the powerful forces at work within these Rays. All of us flow into conscious Life upon one of these Rays, and our entire Life experience is influenced by the Ray through which we descended. In Holy Scripture, the Seven Rays are called the 'seven spirits before the Throne.'

The First Ray is the way of Leadership; the Second Ray is the way of Education; the Third Ray is the way of Philosophy; the Fourth Ray is the way of the Arts; the Fifth Ray is the way of Science; the Sixth Ray is the way of Devotion; and the Seventh Ray is the way of Ceremony. The Esoteric Colours of the Rays are: (1) Red; (2) Light Blue; (3) Green; (4) Yellow; (5) Indigo; (6) Rose; (7) Violet.

It is important to note that the Brotherhood is *not* called: Brotherhood of the *Seventh Ray*. The designation is plural: Brotherhood of the *Seven Rays*. We might ask: If the Brotherhood is working with the Amethystine Order, which is the Seventh Ray, why is it given a name which includes all the Rays of Life? This is a good question, but you will remember that we have already said that each Student of Life at the Monastery must weave a tapestry which symbolizes the Spiritual Life of the Brotherhood. And each Student must accomplish this by weaving his own Ray as if it were a single thread into the whole cloth of the tapestry. The result is that the finished product combines all the Rays of all the Students; the spiritual tapestry of Brotherhood Life is warm, harmonious and vibrant, because each of the Seven Great Rays of Life finds its place in correct correspondence with every other Ray.

This tapestry is more than just symbolical expression or representation, for during the Ceremonies in the Temple of Illumination and the Golden Sun Disc at the Brotherhood, there is a *literal tapestry* on the wall above the Altar of the Pure Maxin Light, the Flame of Illumination. The scenes upon it change according to the thoughts, actions and deeds of the members of the Brotherhood. If all is not in physical, mental and spiritual harmony at the Monastery, it will appear instantly on the tapestry, and some scene will portray the condition symbolically. It is the Brotherhood of the *Seven Rays* because the essence of all Seven is utilized together to bring about the Illumination of Mankind through the Illumination Flame. Of course, all the other Inner Retreats are also working under the Seven Rays, but rather than blending all of them into one force, they each operate under a specific Ray. In this way, the Brotherhood or Focus of Wisdom at Lake Titicaca is unique. We have mentioned before that the Brotherhood of the Seven Rays is also known as the Brotherhood of Illumination. This is for several reasons, the main one being that Lake Titicaca, is the Focus of the Illumination Flame. Lord Muru spoke of this on July 20, 1957, when he said:

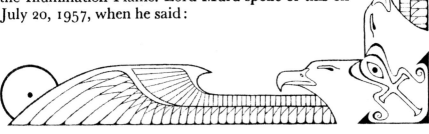

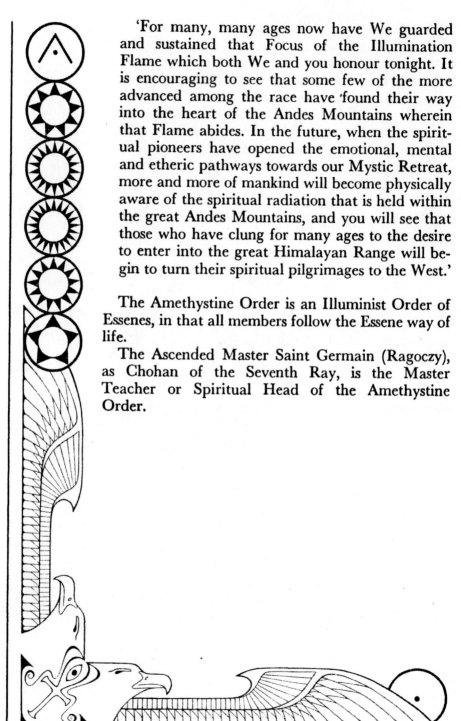

'For many, many ages now have We guarded and sustained that Focus of the Illumination Flame which both We and you honour tonight. It is encouraging to see that some few of the more advanced among the race have 'found their way into the heart of the Andes Mountains wherein that Flame abides. In the future, when the spiritual pioneers have opened the emotional, mental and etheric pathways towards our Mystic Retreat, more and more of mankind will become physically aware of the spiritual radiation that is held within the great Andes Mountains, and you will see that those who have clung for many ages to the desire to enter into the great Himalayan Range will begin to turn their spiritual pilgrimages to the West.'

The Amethystine Order is an Illuminist Order of Essenes, in that all members follow the Essene way of life.

The Ascended Master Saint Germain (Ragoczy), as Chohan of the Seventh Ray, is the Master Teacher or Spiritual Head of the Amethystine Order.

THE ABBEY: LORD MURU'S PRIMARY OUTER RETREAT

ON NOVEMBER 13, 1955, Maha Chohan spoke of Lake Titicaca along with Shamballa, Luxor, Darjeeling, and the Cities of Saint John as Retreats and Sanctuaries of the Great White Brotherhood. Of course, there are many more throughout the world.

On April 12, 1957, Sanat Kumara reported that all the Retreats and Sanctuaries of the Great White Brotherhood had been lifted into a higher spiritual vibration in association with the Celestial Host of the Hierarchy. This concerned the Monastery of the Brotherhood of the Seven Rays at Lake Titicaca. After many centuries of service devoted to the uplifting of mankind, this Inner Retreat of Aramu-Muru had reached a Spiritual Graduation Day. Koot Hoomi Lal Singh (Master Kuthumi) was appointed to act as spokesman for all the Retreats. The action of lifting the Sanctuaries through the authority of the Twenty-Four Elders of our Solar System now permits a greater expansion of work between the Hierarchy and the Retreats that act as intermediate spiritual agencies between man of the Outer world

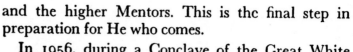

and the higher Mentors. This is the final step in preparation for He who comes.

In 1956, during a Conclave of the Great White Brotherhood, where the banners of all the Inner Retreats were unfurled, it was decided that these Retreats would immediately set up Outer Retreats as a new expression of their service to mankind. Dedicated individuals who would journey as pilgrims to these Outer Retreats were not to be 'called out from among them' to save their physical forms. They were to be gathered together for a divine mission, but not to a place of safety alone, for the power of the Holy Spirit will sustain His servants in time of catastrophe. Formerly, the Outer Retreats had been various groups in the Outer world who were giving forth the words of the Masters of the Hierarchy through meetings, lectures, publications and so on. But now it was desired that there be Retreats that were not as secretive as the Inner Retreats, and yet not associated so much with the world of materialism as the then existing Outer Retreats. The solution to this problem was to have Outer Retreats authorized by each Inner Retreat of the Great White Brotherhood, that would be located near their respective governing body (Retreat.) In such Outer Sanctuaries, Students of Life would follow a monastic way of life similar to that of the Inner Sanctuaries. They would be removed from the world to live in places of peace and solitude, yet they would not be completely removed because they would be sending out reports and making periodic journeys to other lands. They would be closer to the Inner Retreats and the Mentors than ever before. This decision was necessary in order to prepare for impending catastrophe and the eventual landing of the Masters from space. Years ago, man had made the world at large aware of the

Masters and the Mystery Schools by the establishment of certain metaphysical societies and groups. Gradually, a closer association was necessary as the Truths began to penetrate deeper into the national consciousness of every country on Earth. The Students of Truth were closely approaching the various Inner Retreats to which they were connected by a Ray, a Teacher. Now that Outer Retreats were to be established in close proximity to the Inner Retreats, another step in this development took place. The next step will be for those qualified in matters of Spirit from such Outer Retreats to make the final journey to the Inner Sanctuary. This is an indication that events on the Earth are culminating rapidly. When the brothers from interstellar space land, they will be confronted by the *Remnant* that remains, and this *Remnant* will be gathered together in the various locations where the Inner Retreats of the Great White Brotherhood are to be found on the planet's surface.

1956 was an important Spiritual year because of *three* decisions made by the Spiritual Hierarchy:

1. Age-old secrets and Truths would be revealed for the *first time* to the outer world of the profane.
2. Outer Retreats located near Inner Sanctuaries were authorized, and the call sent out to 'come out from among them.'
3. It was decided that in 1957, all the Inner Retreats would be lifted into a new vibration in closer association with the Hierarchy.

Aramu-Muru (God Meru) announced in 1956 to those Students of the Outer World who were members of the Brotherhood of the Seven Rays that he was authorizing an Outer Retreat to be set up in a hidden valley in Peru, and that this Sanctuary was to be

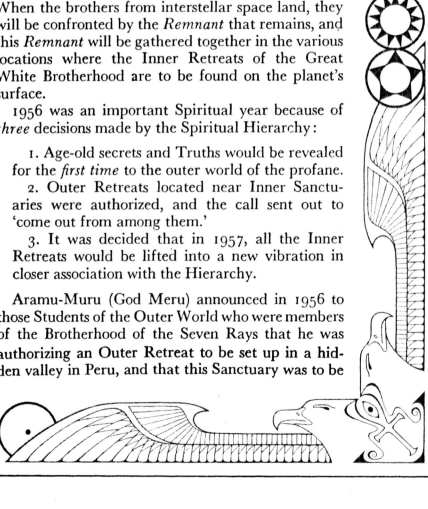

north of the Monastery, its governing body, at Lake Titicaca. The Brotherhood was to have, henceforward, three outlets for its service:

1. The *Monastery*, Lake Titicaca. (*Inner* Retreat.)

2. The *Abbey*, the Hidden Valley, Peru. (Primary Outer Retreat known as an *Intermediate* Sanctuary.)

3. *Priories*. (Various groups not 'brought out from among them' because of their being needed in the world of materialism as agents of distribution for the words of the Great White Brotherhood. They would serve as Secondary *Outer* Retreats.)

As we mentioned before, a few members of the Cyclopean Race did not leave the Earth when the rest of their fellow beings achieved the Theta Universe, but remained behind on our planet because of certain karmic conditions they had to overcome; they were to act as Mentors for hu-man who would come.

As of April 12, 1957, when Sanat Kumara reported that all of the Inner Retreats and Sanctuaries of the Great White Brotherhood had been raised to a higher level of spiritual vibration, the Cyclops who had stayed behind on Earth were at last free to join their Race, the Elder Race or Els. Therefore, Aramu-Muru was released from his position as Spiritual Head (Abbot) of the Monastery. He would continue as Master Teacher of the Brotherhood from a new more ascended position. A certain Brother John (Master John) was appointed to fill the created vacancy as Abbot of the Monastery. Thus, there were no more Cyclops on the Earth in physical form. All of them had, at last, earned and learned the great secret of the *Ninety Degree Phase Shift* and passed into the Universe of Timelessness.

After Lord Muru returned from the conclave of 1956, he immediately put into action those plans which would bring about the organization of the Primary Outer (Intermediate) Retreat as soon as possible. Those members of the Brotherhood in the outer world sold their material possessions, left their places of work and friends, and on December 2, 1956, they began the journey to Lima. From there, most of the cities of Peru were visited and many little-known mountainous areas were searched with the hope that the hidden valley, the future home of Lord Muru's Primary Outer Retreat, would be found. The Mentors guided well, but some of those who had come found themselves incompatible with the Call and Mission, and returned to the United States. Others went on to discover the hidden valley and began the work that had been decreed by the Great White Brotherhood in 1956.

The pilgrims had been given several signs so that they might recognize their Retreat. Briefly, these were:

An area of magnificent natural beauty; a place of peace and tranquillity where blood has never been shed; a location with abundant, clean, pure water; a near-by rushing stream or river; a place where vegetables and fruits could be grown in soil uncontaminated by chemical fertilizers and sprays; a land of happy, contented people who are apart from the Outer world, yet in it.

In February 1957 two Brothers of the Abbey who had come from the United States were in a town of the High Andes where they had been directed by Lord Muru. They were told by their Mentors that

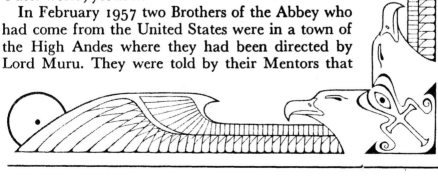

they would be contacted by a man who would lead them to their hidden valley. A few days later, the man appeared and they journeyed with him many miles to the east over great Andean passes filled with snow, where howling, bitter winds sweep the barren land.

The way to the valley was over narrow mountain roads where landslides are common. Is this not like the individual's Spiritual Path which is like a razor's edge, full of hazards as one travels through Life?

There is only one way to reach this valley and that is over the single narrow trail. After long hours of travel, the Brothers arrived at a small village perched high on a fantastic precipice. Above them towered the majestic snow-capped Andes. At the cold village there was a long delay while mules were prepared for the descent into the hidden valley which lay thousands of feet directly below the tiny sky village. All were wrapped in native Quechua woollen ponchos and caps, and finally began the descent in a cold, steady rain. Gradually the climate and the scenery changed. It was as though one were watching winter fade into summer. The rain stopped . . . it became warmer, the woollen clothing was soon discarded and shirt sleeves were in order. The snow and ice that had been so evident just a short time before completely disappeared, and the Brothers felt they were actually living the story of the *Lost Horizon*.

This was, indeed, a Shan-Gri-La, a hidden valley away from the cares of our chaotic planet. Yet, it was a place where a great work could be accomplished in its peaceful atmosphere, where blood has never been shed, and where Quechua-speaking Indians, descendants of the great Inca Sun Empire, live quietly in a semi-tropical paradise.

On all sides of the valley, hundreds of beautiful

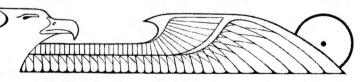

waterfalls dash down great rock walls to bring clear, pure water from the Andean glaciers into the valley. And there was a great and rushing river, a beautiful thing to behold as it wound its way through the entire length of the valley like a shining silver thread.

The Brothers soon learned that practically anything could be grown in the valley. A place where temperate zone products grow side by side with those of the tropical zone! Corn, beans, squash, yucca, peas, beets, carrots, lettuce, cabbage, papayas, mangos, cherimoya—a fabulous fruit nearly 100 per cent protein — potatoes, avocados, tomatoes, bananas, lemons, oranges, etc., grow in abundance, and these are only a few of the fruits and vegetables available. The planting season is throughout the year and no chemical fertilizers or sprays are used; everything is grown organically and naturally.

The two Brothers of the Abbey instantly recognized this valley as the future home of Lord Muru's Primary Outer Retreat.

The Brothers left the hidden valley reluctantly, for the atmosphere of peace that hangs over the place is powerful and unforgettable. Picture, if you can, the narrow, winding foot and mule paths that have never known the brutal wheels of modern vehicles, the llama trains, always picturesque with the bright coloured yarn 'owner's markers' in the animal ears, the silent, friendly Quechua Indian who awaits the appearance of his reincarnated Inca ancestors, when they will again be led in a new Inca Sun Empire of a Golden Dawn on Earth. These people, although isolated in this hidden valley, know what is going on in the world today, and patiently await the return of *Viracocha*, the Great White Brother.

Students of Life have now entered the valley and there is a fine building housing the Abbey along with

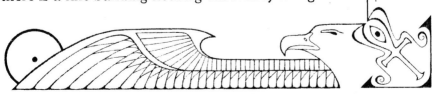

the Scriptorium (Library) and the Temple of Life. All Students follow a Monastic Way of Life as directed by the Great White Brotherhood. The Abbey operates under the direct authority and guidance of the Monastery. All members belong to the Amethystine Order, an Illuminist Order of Essenes. They serve under the Seventh or Violet (Purple) Ray. The name of the Abbey in the ancient Quechua language of the Incas is *Intihuaci*, House of the Sun.

So-called rules and regulations are followed at the Abbey so that all Students of Life may partake of a great Spiritual unfoldment and experience. The Brotherhood does not believe that the following way of life is necessary for salvation, or even that such a routine would be right for all people. The routine at the Abbey has been developed to bring about certain Spiritual Illumination for advanced Students on the Path of Cosmic Understanding. The following requirements are for Novices ready to enter Lord Muru's Primary Outer Retreat, the Abbey of the Brotherhood:

The Student of Life applying for entry into the Abbey must, first of all, be *seeking* and *serving* Truth, and living a clean and upright life. He must have a theoretical understanding of the Great Path. There are absolutely no restrictions as to age, sex, marital status, race, religious affiliation, nor is the Brotherhood interested in anyone's past record. The important thing is that the individual Student, at the time of application, is desiring Truth above all else. There is no religion higher than Truth!

The Student must be aware of and accept the Cosmic Christ and believe that this Christ as God *came in the flesh* to mentor the Earth and that this same Christ will return again soon *in the flesh*.

'Simplify simply.' The way of life at the Abbey is

well defined by David Thoreau's famous words. This is of utmost importance in the daily life.

While, in reality, there are no degrees to put one Student above another, there is a classification at the Abbey which is for work designation: Applicant; Novice; Friar; Monk; Prior (Prioress); Abbot (Abbess.)

The Essene way of life is followed by all Students. There are regular periods of fasting, meditation and contemplation at the Abbey. Students are mendicants (monks with vows of poverty.) The Sacred Communal Meal or Supper of the Essenes is taken daily, and the Novice undergoes Water Baptism by complete immersion before he becomes a Friar, and the Friar undergoes Sacred Anointing with Oil before he becomes a Monk of the Order.

Students rise at dawn and return to their own quarters at sunset after meditation in the Temple of Life.

No narcotics (tobacco, medicines, etc.) or stimulants, such as coffee, tea or chocolate are used at the Abbey. Certain beneficial herb teas are used, however. No intoxicants, either in medicines or foods or beverages are used. No animal products are eaten. All Students adhere to strict vegetarianism and food is mostly raw, and taken from individual wooden bowls. Pure honey is used. No processed foods, canned foods, chemicalized or bleached foods are eaten. Only organically grown, natural foods are consumed and which are free from poisons. Most Students prefer a diet of raw, natural fruits and nuts. Our body is the *Temple of God.* 'Thou shalt not kill' and 'Live and let live' are principles to live by at the Abbey.

Monastic garments, while worn at the Abbey, are not compulsory. White or unbleached simple cloth-

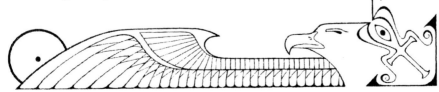

ing is used by the Students. Slacks, shorts, jeans, etc., are not worn. However, this does not apply to Students on missions where such clothing is necessary.

No jewellery or cosmetics are permitted. This includes wedding and engagement rings, but does *not* include wrist watches, buckles, glasses, etc.

Hair is worn long by Students of both sexes. Men may wear beards if they wish, but it is not required.

Pets are not recommended.

Children of all ages are welcomed at the Abbey. There is a fine programme for them of study, recreation and meditation.

All Students are expected to take care of themselves financially. Living in Peru is very reasonable, and in the hidden valley even more so.

Those with serious physical and mental disorders are not encouraged to come to the Abbey. In the journey to the valley, high altitudes are encountered, and there are rigours in the trip that would make it impossible for some individuals. Such can serve the Christ Light where they are and guide the Master's sheep in the dawn of a New Age.

The family unit is retained at the Abbey since families live away from the main building in private locations. Therefore, family life is preserved, while, at the same time, all Students become a part of the Brotherhood Community. Single men and women may share their quarters with members of their own sex if they so desire.

The entire experience of a Student of Life at the Abbey, the Primary Outer Retreat of Lord Muru, is one of initiation into physical, mental, and spiritual illumination. This initiation consists of: dedication; purification; discipline; instruction; service. No one will be saved because they join the Abbey or because they follow the monastic way of life of the Brother-hood. However, the rewards to the individual student in the form of universal lessons learned, are great.

The Symbol or Seal of the Monastery is the Pink Rose whose colour is representative of the Illumination Flame. Pink Roses are always symbolic of the Messengers of Aramu-Muru. This beautiful Rose is superimposed on a Disc of Gold, for gold represents the other colour of the Illumination Flame and, also, the Golden Sun Disc of Mu.

The Symbol or Seal of the Abbey is the Golden Sun Disc of Mu, with Twelve projecting Rays which stand for the Twelve Inner and the Twelve Outer Planets of our Solar System. The Rays also symbolize the Twelve Lords. Six of these Rays are shorter than the others, because six is the number representative of world service. Superimposed on the Sun Disc is the ancient *ankh* or *crux ansata*. This was the Cross of Life in Ancient Egypt and stands for Life Eternal. This symbol is used because the Primary Outer Retreat is actively engaged in demonstrating to man that nothing ever really dies. Above the *ankh* is the All-Seeing Eye of the Infinite One who is the Divine Guiding light of all Retreats.

The *Banner* or *Standard* of the Abbey contains a purple field which represents the Amethystine Order. Upon it is placed a Golden Sun Disc out of which project Seven Rays, each Ray ending in a Flame. The Disc, of course, stands for the original Sun Disc of Mu that is now in the subterranean Temple of the Inner Retreat, and also because the Quechua name for the Abbey is *Intihuaci*, House of the Sun. The Seven Rays stand for the Brotherhood of the Seven Rays and for the *Seven Root Races* (and Seven Sub-Races of each Root Race,) belonging to the Earth's evolution. The Flames stand for the Illumination

Flame in the Temple of Illumination. This Temple, also houses the Golden Sun Disc of Mu, and is located in a cave-like chamber or subterranean hall near the Monastery. Every Hierarch, every Ascended Being and every Inner or Outer Retreat or Sanctuary has its own symbol and banner.

As we have said before, individual Students of all races and creeds are going to be gathered together at the Outer Retreats of the Great White Brotherhood, where they will form a great spiritual and philosophical Congress. Research work has begun at the Abbey in radionics, including a new method that *exactly* dates the past and objects from the past—a true Time Scanner; nutrition and organic gardening; metaphysics; linguistics; anthropology and archaeology; historical research; investigation into the UFO field and contact with visitors from space who belong to the *Confederation* which is actively assisting the Great White Brotherhood at the present time; Sun and Light Energy; work with children of all ages; better methods of Meditation and Contemplation; botanical research to discover new miracle plants and herbs. Prominent New Age leaders and organizations the world over have been invited to co-operate and share in the Abbey's intensive programme.

If you feel the Call, if you would give up all and come to a hidden valley, indeed, an enchanted valley known to the ancient dwellers in the land as Place of the Flowers where dwell the Little People of legend, then come, bringing only your souls!

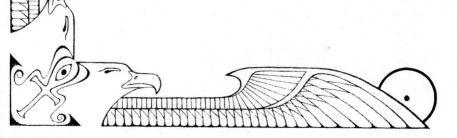

The ORDER of the RED HAND

THE SCRIPTORIUM of the Monastery is under the direction of its Prior, Brother Philip. This chamber houses documents and records, codices and parchments of the world's greatest and most ancient civilizations. Rome, Greece, Egypt and Babylonia, Crete and China, Tibet and Troy, Atlantis, Mu and Adoma, and even earlier. From such hidden libraries as this will come forth from all the Inner Retreats of the Great White Brotherhood, the old and *true history* of our planet and its great revelation for modern man. Man will be greatly surprised when he discovers history as it *really* happened! Previously, the dark forces have written history as they wished it to be interpreted.

The ancient *Order of the Red Hand* has worked throughout Earth's history in the preservation of the Secret Wisdom, the Arcane Knowledge. Members of this Order are guardians of Earth's vast storehouse of treasure more precious than gold or gems. It is they who hold the secrets that are man's heritage in South America.

This continent was not merely a vast area colonized on its west coast by Lemurians, and on its east by Atlanteans. While it is true that those two great civilizations of the Atlantic and Pacific Oceans did

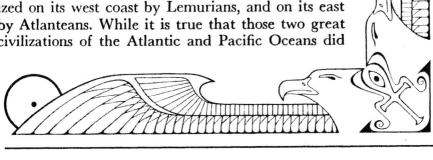

colonize parts of South America, this was only a few thousand years ago just before the final destruction of the Motherlands. What, then, existed before Atlantean and Lemurian cultural influence on the great South American Continent?

On May 27, 1957, an ancient secret, heretofor known only to the highest teachers, was revealed to the Outer world through the Abbey. It was appropriate that this information be first given from South America where the events related took place in the dim past.

The Great White Brotherhood decided that it was time for such secrets to be given out in conformity with its three decisions of 1956. The startling secret was that South America existed side by side with Atlantis and Mu as a third great world civilization. Not just a colony but a civilization in its own right, an Amazonian Empire which was culturally ahead of its more famous and well-known neighbours in the nearby oceans. Its architecture was more magnificent, its science outshadowed all others while its people were physically the most beautiful upon the Earth. In many ways it acted as Mentor to the kings, priests and teachers of the two better known Lost Continents of Earth.

It differs from them in yet another respect. While they both sank under the ocean waves, it remained always above the water, shrouded in dense jungle, waiting for re-discovery in an age when man would lose his hunger for gold alone and would not seek this Empire's material wealth but would search out its greater treasures, the keys to a more abundant and longer life, knowledge that would eventually present the Universe itself at man's feet.

Yet, is it not a Lost Continent also? It may just as well have been under water, for few men have sought its truths, and those that did have either disappeared in the Green Hell of the jungle or the forgetfulness of Time itself. Now, in the fullness of that time, the Hierarchy has decreed that the 'Secret Places of the Most High' shall give up their Knowledge to a *'Remnant'* that will remain upon the Earth in the days immediately following world-wide catastrophe. That same *Remnant* will use this ancient wisdom in a New World that will once again be brought into the Interplanetary Brotherhood of our Solar System. Mankind will, indeed, begin its eternal march across Time and the Stars.

Records of Mu's history and downfall, of the fate of Atlantis, and of the secrets of the enlightened Amazonian Empire known in legends as Paititi and of the Cyclops who came to Earth a billion years ago, and of the inhabitants of interstellar space, exist in special hidden chambers in the great Lost Cities of the unexplored interior of South America.

While it is true that our brothers from space will teach us much in our New Age, they also tell us that it is far better if we regain once more the so-called lost knowledge of the Earth's Golden or Saturnian Age when men spoke with the gods and with the angels. They tell us that such knowledge is our true heritage, and belongs to all Truth-seeking men of Earth. It is a Divine Gift from the Eternal Father, and the Son is now ready for his inheritance. Therefore, we need not rely only on great intelligence that is extra-terrestrial, for we have our own knowledge that will lead us forward to where we can stand side by side with our planetary brothers and sisters. Man can look to the skies of Earth for guidance at this time, but for scientific knowledge he can look to her secret places, where Mother Earth will bring forth from her womb a Knowledge that has been protected

and cared for within her for thousands of years, and which will shortly be born unto the Outer world of men. Verily, even now the pains of labour begin.

The *Order of the Red Hand* is as old as man upon the face of the Earth. Everywhere, archaeologists find representations of a human hand painted red. It exists in abundance on cave walls throughout Europe, in cave dwellings in North America, and is found on many of the walls of the Mayan Temples in Yucatan, Mexico. The hand itself is a mystical symbol of great antiquity, and the mysteries it represents are still incorporated in the secret lodge ceremonies of today. Scientists have wondered why the *Red Hand* is so much in evidence among world peoples. And simply because they do not know nor have a better explanation, they say that it is only proof that the ancients were good doodlers and dabblers.

But, to you who are Students of Light, the *Red Hand* was and is much more than that. It stands for the preservation of all that *was* and *is* good and true, while its opposite, the Black Hand, stands for the destruction of the Arcane Knowledge that has been accumulated over many centuries. For example, it was the force of the Black Hand that destroyed the Alexandrian Library, but it was the efforts of the *Red Hand* that prevented total destruction and secured the most important documents in hidden chambers so that only copies or unimportant manuscripts went up in the flames started by Caesar.

The members of the *Order of the Red Hand* are found in many of the Inner Retreats and Mystery Schools throughout the Earth, and they are the appointed guardians over the Secret Places of the Most High. This ancient Order is now in charge of the expeditionary group of the Abbey. Many projects are under way, including research with the rediscovered Lost Writing of the Pre-Incas and of the Empire of Paititi, complete exploration and mapping of the Great Wall of Peru which is similar to the Great Wall of China and was absolutely unknown until 1931 when it was viewed from the air. This Wall is far older than the Incas or the Chimus before them. Why it was built and the story behind it is fabulous. Another project deals with the re-discovery of the Solar Light Energy used by the Pre-Incas and later by the Incas, who copied them. Yet another project deals with the re-discovery of the Lost Capital of ancient Paititi itself. Already much has been done to bring this about. There are also other projects dealing with the underground tunnel system of the ancient Pre-Incas. The Abbey has received the assistance of several South American universities and museums and co-operative scientists. This is invaluable when dealing with the Outer world so that the most benefit can be derived from the discoveries made.

This then, is really a quest for the *Red Hand*, a quest for the Truth about man and why he finds himself upon the Red Planet Earth, what he must learn while he is here, and where he is going in the New Age now dawning. Although, at first, it seems strange, Lost Cities of South America and the UFOs belonging to arriving space visitors, are connected, and both play a vital role in the present work of the ancient *Order of the Red Hand*!

LOST WORLDS and the COMING of the SPACE-MASTERS

W E HAVE ALREADY spoken of the legacy for man hidden in the South American jungles that is beyond his wildest imagination. In ancient record chambers scientific knowledge will be found and utilized in the New Age, secrets of a very remote past will be the incentive for magnificent development in a newer world. The cities of the fabulous Amazonian Empire, which antedated other world civilizations, belong to another Lost Continent but, unlike Atlantis and Mu, this Continent is not buried *under* any ocean, but instead, it is buried *behind* miles of Green Hell that constitute the South American jungles. These cities have *never* been under water; their records therefore are well preserved in their final resting places in the vast libraries of forgotten Paititi. Countless treasures were brought to Paititi by informed priest-scientists when it was known that both Lemuria and Atlantis were definitely doomed to oblivion. What an inheritance will be found in areas where now only the sound of the monkey and the call of the bird are known—the combined knowledge of the three greatest empires the world has ever known.

Early in June 1957, the Expeditionary Group of

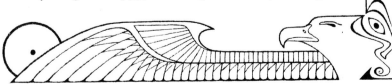

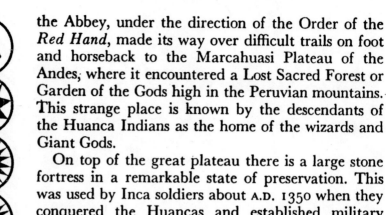

the Abbey, under the direction of the Order of the *Red Hand*, made its way over difficult trails on foot and horseback to the Marcahuasi Plateau of the Andes, where it encountered a Lost Sacred Forest or Garden of the Gods high in the Peruvian mountains. This strange place is known by the descendants of the Huanca Indians as the home of the wizards and Giant Gods.

On top of the great plateau there is a large stone fortress in a remarkable state of preservation. This was used by Inca soldiers about A.D. 1350 when they conquered the Huancas and established military occupation of the entire region. There are many stone *chulpas* or burial tombs surrounding the fortress, all of which have been robbed. After the murder of the Inca Emperor Atahualpa at Cajamarca, Peru, the Spanish arrived at Marcahuasi and destroyed the ancient mummy bundles to satisfy their lust for the yellow metal. Today, only a few bones remain in each tomb. An ancient burial cave, thousands of feet above a valley, proved to be very important for it contained an unopened tomb that, by some miracle, had not yet been violated. There were countless mummies inside, but the discovery is insignificant when compared with the fantastically ancient sculptured stones of the Marcahuasi Plateau.

This plateau is 12,000 feet above sea level, and is shrouded in fog most of the year, but during the months between May and September there is a bright sun and it becomes a delightful place, although very cold at night. The many and great sculptured stones represent an important key to the world's ancient mysteries. Birds and animals from lions and elephants to camels and penguins which never existed in South America have been carved in gigantic proportions. All human races appear to be

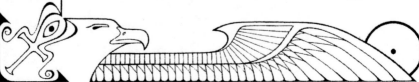

represented and many great stone heads bear resemblance to those found on famous Easter Island in the Pacific.

Many ancient religions are symbolized by beautiful and finely carved sphinxes, faces and figures of forgotten gods and goddesses. The figures are immense and from scientific calculations, it is believed they were made by a race of giant men at least twelve feet tall. It is not yet known for certain whether they belonged to the Cyclopean Race or not, but the strange dimensional quality of the carvings is an indication that this may be so.

There are many legends that exist among present-day natives in South America—the Incas spoke of the giants, also—that tell of the giant blond men who once inhabited the continent. These are not ordinary gigantic statues or figures, for when the sunlight, or the moonlight, strikes them at a certain angle, you see things it is impossible to see at any other time. The features change as you view them at different times, under different conditions, and from different angles. Most of the figures have three or four eyes, but no matter where you observe them from, they always seem to present only two. If you are not at a given, fixed point of observation you do not see the statues as they were intended to be seen. Therefore, we had to locate the elevated platforms near the figures that were used by the makers for observational purposes.

The figures are carved out of granite, but are now badly eroded. Yet, they are magnificent in their execution even today, and it takes your breath away to contemplate them and their creators. Who were these giants? Where did they come from? Where did they go to? We will answer such questions through our research at the Abbey.

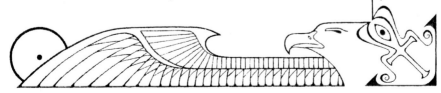

The figures cover an area of several square miles, and reports from other parts of South America indicate that they are to be found elsewhere, although not in such a state of isolation or profusion as at Marcahuasi.

There are several altars that were obviously made to be used by giant creatures, but even more startling is the fact that something out of this world seems to be hovering over the plateau. Almost all the time one can hear a very odd humming sound coming from the figures, and this sound is not due to natural causes. You feel you are dealing with something outside of man's ability to understand at the present time, a look into another dimension of Time and Space.

When one takes a photo of a carved figure of a very old man and observes the negative, it appears not as an old man, but as a young and handsome youth. Who could carve stone so that at certain angles shapes will change and cast shadows into valleys, where, as the light changes, strange creatures move as if alive?

This race of giant beings used natural objects that seemed to bear resemblance to known animals, and then, by carving them, they enhanced the setting. The result is something that appears to be born right out of the soil. This was a Sacred Forest where no one ever lived, used as it was exclusively for scientific religious purposes. Science and religion were then joined together in Truth as they will be again in the New Age. It is perhaps the last Sacred Forest that remains nearly intact and unmolested by modern man. It is possible that Marcahuasi was used by the race that later came to be known as Ls. The Huanca Indians still venerate Huari who was a Hercules of their legends—a giant. It appears that a memory of the giants persisted to linger in the mythology of the Huancas and their Huari must have originally been a great leader of the giant race. The Huancas still celebrate strange rituals in hidden areas near the plateau, rituals no white man has ever seen. Until some years ago, the rites were celebrated at Marca-huasi itself.

The most startling fact of all disclosed by the Abbey research is that when Peruvian Government aerial photos of the plateau are studied carefully, one can see definite, gigantic figures that are visible only from the air. Does this mean that the giants had airships? Were the figures, as seen from the air, markers or symbols of some sort for ships arriving from interstellar space or other nearby planets? Marcahuasi will prove to be an important area for further research in relation to the Cyclopean Race and the coming of the Masters from Space.

During the first part of July 1957, the Expeditionary Group of the Abbey, moved eastwards towards the legendary Paititi. The vast wilderness country east of Cuzco was penetrated in the region of the Rio Alto Madre de Dios. Many difficulties were encountered by the expedition, but great success attended the venture. The usual jungle inhabitants were obvious by their presence in great numbers. Vampire bats, jaguars, tapirs, giant ants, poisonous snakes and other creatures proved to be bothersome, but they did not hinder the progress of the research in the unexplored territory near the headwaters of the Rio Sinkibenia. Kinship with all life was practised and this may have had something to do with the fact that the members of the expedition had small difficulty with animals considering the dangers of the area and the fact that no one carried a gun.

Hundreds of times dangerous rapids in swift-mov-

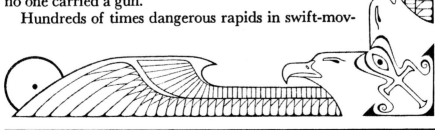

ing rivers had to be crossed, and all in all, over 200 kilometres were covered through swamps and thick jungle growth that proved to be an almost impenetrable wall as we cut our way through it with machetes. When there were no trails of any kind, we had to walk up the middle of the rivers or use the rock beaches where they existed. We could not possibly enter this unknown land during the rainy season for then the rivers are very high and anyone on foot could not penetrate any great distance.

Our destination the first part of July 1957 was a low group of mountains which are really only the last vestiges of the Andes to the west. It appeared at a distance like a Lost World of fiction fame, great green mounds shrouded in fog and mist, a world that impressed us with majesty and mystery. Foot travel was difficult and slow.

This may be an unknown land to modern man, but it is a land that was not forgotten by his Creator, for it is magnificently beautiful. We came to this area because of the countless legends among South American tribes that somewhere in this vicinity is a great Lost Stone City of the Ancient Ones. The Spanish explorer, Juan Alvarez Maldonado, conducted an expedition into the area of the Alto Madre de Dios in the sixteenth century and looked for this same city. However, he never visited the area of our destination, for it is still unknown.

A few years ago, a Piro Indian was in the same area looking for his run-away Machiguenga Indian wife. In the chain of low mountains near the headwaters of two unknown rivers he came upon a stone roadway. He followed it to a great city of magnificent stone houses, plazas, and temples. No Inca or Spaniard had ever visited these remains. Why? Because this Lost City is only one of many that belonged to the ancient Amazonian Empire of Paititi. In the vicinity where the Piro Indian made his discovery, legends spoke of a strange Lost Doorway or Portal to an antediluvian world. (Not really an entrance-way, but the stone face of an enormous cliff covered with writings which the tribes said was unknown to them although they have lived in the area for hundreds upon hundreds of years.)

On July 10, 1957, we discovered this fabled Doorway or Rock of the Writing in unknown territory on the Rio Sinkibenia. We were very near an unknown, wild tribe that had never been visited by civilized men before. They do not desire contact with the outside world which they have heard about from other visiting Indians. The Abbey will continue its research in this important area and will pass through the village of this tribe in order to attempt to reach the Lost Stone City. The people of this city carved the figures and hieroglyphics on the Rock of the Writing.

Many drawings and photographs were made that year of the thousands of petroglyphs that are not crude rock carvings made by stoneage man, but genuine hieroglyphics of a highly advanced and ancient race. The glyphs are in the form of Scroll Writing of Atlantis and Mu, and are the record of the people of the Lost Stone City. They are related to the world's oldest languages and they cover an area, on the face of the stone cliff, eighty-five feet in length and about eight feet in height. Many appear to be related to Mayan and Aztec glyphs, and there is even an attempt at bas-relief in some carved figures.

One figure of a young man in a great helmet shows him pointing to the west. We believe he is pointing in the direction of the Lost City, whose priest-scien-

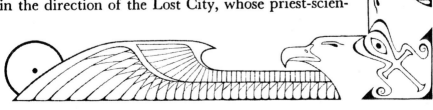

tists recorded important historical happenings on the great stone cliff. There are similar city records which are to be found in the Temples of Egypt. Three other rocks of writings were located and these will be studied in the future during other expeditions. The Expeditionary Group returned down the Rio Sinki-benia on a balsa raft they had to build themselves, and completed the rest of the journey by Indian canoe and by foot.

The fact that the hieroglyphics are authentic writing is a discovery of major importance in South America, for it is believed that the Incas and Pre-Incas had no form of writing whatsoever. At the Abbey, students will continue their research on the glyphs.

Besides this discovery, many legends were collected from the little-known Machiguenga tribe of the area. These legends speak in detail of the catastrophes that overtook the world during the final destruction of Lemuria and Atlantis. This was, of course, during the time when ancient Tiahuanaco was lifted from sea level to the barren heights, and the Andes were born. It was a time when Aramu-Muru was above the angry sea in his airship heading for South America with the records and the Golden Sun Disc of Mu. Great earthquakes occurred throughout all of the South American Continent. Cities like Tiahuan-aco on the coast were most affected. These coastal centres of population were Lemurian Colonial Cities, while the Lost Stone Cities farther to the east were much more ancient, belonging to the Amazonian Empire, and had nothing to do with Lemuria's col-onization plans. They were located in an area that suffered milder damage and the buildings were either not ruined, or only partially so.

Other legends of the Machiguenga tribe speak of

the time when their ancestors were in communication with the *people of the sky,* and the Machiguenga language is not a language of savages, and proves that these people have degenerated to their present state due to the destruction of the Amazonian Empire. However, if the cities were not totally destroyed during the catastrophe why did the natives degenerate? It is believed that the Machiguengas and other tribes were not the rulers of the cities, but that they were workers for these people, and that those who governed them were bearded white men. In fact, it is rumoured by the jungle tribes today that such white men in long robes still live and carry on research at the capital of Paititi which is a Lost City of Thirty Citadels, ancient beyond belief when the Incas first came to Peru. The rulers of the Inca Sun Empire searched for this city but never found it. The Spanish conquerors after Pizarro braved death in the wilderness to plunder its immense treasure of gold, silver and jewels. They never even so much as once glimpsed its outer courts. It has been held from the eyes of gold-hungry men, for it has a treasure far more valuable than any yellow metal or gem to adorn the neck or arm of a proud and haughty daughter of the world.

In the towers of the Lost Cities there is a blazing crystal of white light that shines eternally. This, undoubtedly, is the Maxin Light of the ancients and it is connected with the same power that is utilized today by the visitors from space in the UFOs. Many space craft are being reported by the missionaries in the interior of South America, and the Space Confederation has a gigantic base there near the remains of the Lost Cities that existed in magnificence in a time when their ancestors from space landed there and established communication with the priest-

scientists of the cities. Masters from Space sat in great conclaves with Masters of Earth, for was it not a time when men conversed with the gods? In our generation the interplanetary visitors have returned to visit the cities once again.

Master Teachers of the world's Inner Retreats, in co-operation with the Hierarchy of the Great White Brotherhood, are now in communication with the arriving Masters from Space just as they were during the time of Paititi's glory ages ago. Because of the rumours of the white teachers in robes appearing in the jungle even today, it is likely many of the Lost Cities serve as a Focus of Wisdom.

Dear Student of Light can you grasp the vision that the Celestial Hierarchy wants us to know? Can you see the future where Space Men and Space Teachers mingle with Earth men and Earth Teachers to guide the *Remnant* that remains? As catastrophes caused the Arcane Knowledge to be hidden, now they will also cause the same Knowledge to be revealed once again to spiritually hungry man. But fear not these changes in the world. Follow the words of the Master Kirpal Singh Ji Maharaj of Delhi, a living Saint still clothed in a physical form:

There is no need to worry. Each of the Initiates should learn to rise above the body consciousness by regular practices in meditation. No sting of death will be felt. You should do nothing but take sensible precautions (if at all necessary) and devote time regularly in meditation and leave everything else to the Master Power which is overhead each of the Initiates and which is extending all feasible help and protection. Efforts are being made to check the impending catastrophe in Higher Circles. *Master Power is overhead the Initiates and they need not be afraid.*

There are Students of Light now working and serving in the *New World Focus of Illumination* where the *Feminine Aspect* of the *Permanent Ray* enters the Earth. They trod the trails of the mountains and the valleys, and they walk where there are no trails; they know the rivers and lakes, the glaciers and deserts; they are tireless as those Servants of old, yet they have a modern mission in that they must teach a New World. They must present the *true* ancient world to the present so that the future world now appearing as a golden sun on the horizon of our day may inherit its Divine Legacy. These, then, are the Brothers of the Seven Rays—Essenes of the Andes.

TRANSCRIPT of the HIERARCHY

ALL THE MENTORS presented here have been, and continue to be, channelled and recorded at the Scriptorium which is housed in the Abbey, the Primary Outer Retreat or Sanctuary of the Brotherhood of the Seven Rays (Illumination) in the Peruvian Andes.

Some of the Mentors who speak here are Ascended Master Saints, while others are Teachers who still live in a physical form on the Earth and serve in the Mystery Schools of the Great White Brotherhood. Their words are recorded by means of voice channelling of a telepathic nature.

Beloved Sanat Kumara

Beloved, all space is vibrant with love, harmony, and peace, as directed by many men from many spheres. The light of their love is ever growing into a great flame that shall consume all lust, greed, hatred, malice, and shall sweep over the Earth as a great tidal wave.

Long ago, as I witnessed a great Star that appeared in the East, this was the sign unto man of

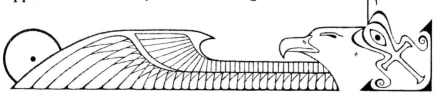

Earth that redemption draweth nigh, that salvation was present.

No soul, no matter how degraded, shall be denied admittance to the great school of life. This is the time when truly the lion shall lie down with the lamb.

On the Earth there is the great confusion of man's mind that causes the turmoil and even the seas boil in hatred; but He came to prove that the troubled waters can be calmed and stilled, the fury of the night winds can be hushed by the raising of one hand, not the raising of a hand to slay and to curse, but the raising of a hand in loving benediction. The Father placed the Earth and all celestial bodies in the heavens. They are created out of spiralling primordial matter for man. Man was to be the god of physical form: man, the highest expression of Deity known in the entire Omniverse.

O, man! realize that you are the highest form of Deity anywhere in the Omniverse. There is nothing beyond you. And in this you are grand; and in this you are the lowest. You are the lowest because you *know* and the other life forms do not know. Therefore, you must be their brother and their servant.

There is life and intelligence in all forms, as ancient man knew. Man alone is not the only thinking being. Every element, every mineral—all forms —have inherent intelligence, and man is their keeper and their elder brother. You are the elder brother of these forms, innumerable forms throughout the Omniverse. It is up to you to raise them to ever higher evolution as they, along with man progress up the worlds to infinite grandeur, to Infinite Light.

The beauty of the age now approaches when all doubts and fears shall be rolled away as a great scroll. And there shall be a great thundering! The heavens are torn asunder! And then man views himself and looks into the mirror of knowing. No longer is there confusion. Man accepts the sceptre of his godhood so that no longer may his progression up the stars be hindered by the darkness of ignorance and superstition. Know this, and in knowing it there must of necessity be sadness; and yet there must be gladness for the beauty that it shall bring.

But now for a moment I do speak on that which impends and is forthcoming. Yes, there can be atomic detonations and cosmic ray bombardments, but these are the effects. What is the cause? The cause of the destruction that shall come upon the Earth is from man's own thinking.

Since the time when the Sons of God came in unto the daughters of men and animal-man appeared upon the Earth he has been striving from beasthood back to angelhood. But faulty thinking shall now break forth as the elements refuse to be regarded as they have been for millennia upon the Earth. The elements! they *are* intelligent life! They are part of the Infinite One, and because they are part of the Infinite One they will not respond to man's negative thinking any longer. And they will rebel, causing great tidal waves and great winds. Millions shall perish! They shall be reborn anew on other worlds appropriate to their level of progression. And because of the *remnant* that must remain, the Earth is purified and raised to a new vibration.

Very soon the winds shall howl, sooner than we can realize. It is already upon us, for I have witnessed it in the plane which is just above that of physical expression upon the Earth, and that means that if it descends one more plane it shall find reality. The fields and the great cities shall be desolate without inhabitant. Can you imagine a great city such as London, New York, Paris, where millions of men and

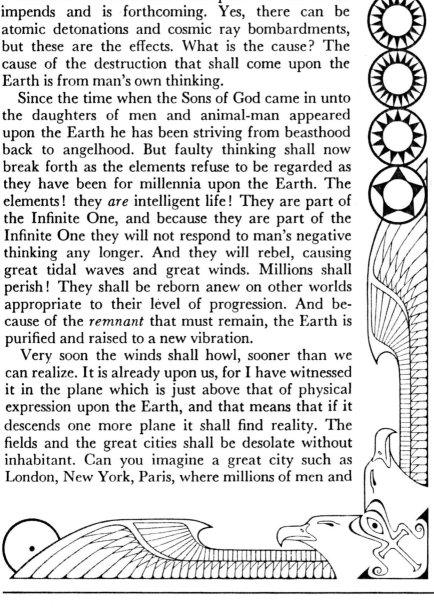

women love, work, and play? Can you imagine a more desolate scene than a city of millions without inhabitant? It is like suddenly the Universe has been deprived of men, for the joy of the Creator is in His highest expression—man. Without man He is without love. Even though man can be His greatest hurt, man also can raise Him to the greatest aspiration. For without man even the Infinite One cannot progress, for why would we limit Him? If man can progress cannot He progress also? Cannot He through His own creation find new thrills in love?

O, man of Earth! if you knew the love that descends to you from spheres innumerable, from minds inviolate! If you would listen you would know. There can be nothing but beauty. From all the catastrophe that shall come only the vision of a beautiful 'rose' shall remain, for man steps forth in a purified light of his own creation.

The forces of the Black Dragon—they can deafen the ears of man to the music of the spheres, to the melodies of the angelic hosts, but yet they have not found power to still the celestial movements for, no matter how powerful their armies, the Moon will still remain to meet the dawn of a new day. And they have not yet learned how to still the melodic song of the brook nor can they in their attainments reach the heights that the eagle can reach in his soaring upwards, as a great prayer that rises from the Earth towards the Infinite Throne, for the eagle is master of the Earth above all of them.

Remember the beauty of Earth is in the creation that you stand upon, from which you derive your nourishment. It is like the bosom of our Father, where we rest our head to regain strength. It is our mother and yet it is our father. The Earth is a beautiful world, vastly more beautiful than some of its neighbours. I have always loved the Earth beyond all other creations, for I see within it a melody that has not yet escaped into the ethers. I see it crying as one *bound*! But it shall not be deprived its celestial song much longer.

No, I say that the Black Dragon, with all its negative force, has not been able to take away from the beauty of the creation. This force has not been able to deny the brook or the world the twilight song. Yea, if they could they would deprive the gentleness of night, the twilight song. I say now is the time when the dusty feet of gods shall become the dust that swirls about their ugly forms. Idle rust, rust must be!

It is truly recorded in the greatest archives of akasha that God did truly provide and man divided. That is the motto of Earth. Man must come back from his multitudinous sins to the One God, for it is not in complexity that we find the Father. It is in simplicity that we find Him.

As you serve, remember each and every one of your fellow-men is deity. Think of each one that you meet not as this man or woman or child but that each one that comes before you *is the Father in essence*. If you would think on Earth of each one as part of the Father, with due respect in that degree, then the Earth's problems would dissolve instantly.

And now the hungry multitudes of Earth are crying for a Saviour who can once again give them the loaves and fishes, who, from a small paltry substance, can feed and satisfy their hunger. They are crying now for the waters of life, for the manna of wisdom. And I say that it is written—it is an edict from the Highest One Himself—that this shall be done, for He has commanded: these are my children; they must be led back to my bosom and they must be fed my substance.

We who hold the Earth in our hand were given her to develop, to cherish, and to bring to fruition. We now see that the harvest shall be ample and the storehouse of the Father will be full for the migration to new grandeur of being.

I would give you a divine commandment for the time immediately ahead: Feed the sheep of God! Give where it is required. Give not of your past glories but give them that which the soul needs. Tell them that there shall be catastrophe! Prepare them for that. But tell them out of this shall come the greater light,—Tell them that, yes, catastrophe comes upon the Earth; for the night cometh when no man can work, and the night is now here—catastrophe, disaster and despair. And the flood gates and the winds shall wash and blow away all the old. It was the spawn of darkness; for it can be endured by all men if they know beyond is rainbow's end, the golden promise of godhood and oneness with our Father.

If you only knew upon worlds without number in space—stars of great majesty and beauty that appear like beautiful gems in the black velvet of the Omniverse—the millions of souls that are crying out, and their voices ring out in a peal of peace towards the Earth. If men were aware of such love and such affection and such direction the problems of Earth would not be problems at all.

Therefore it is your duty to bring them this message which is a two-fold message: a warning to prepare for that which shall come in the waves and the winds; and it is a message secondarily that there are those who care, who are acting as the emissaries of the Infinite One. Tell them they are loved, that they shall be guided as they ask to be guided: 'Ask, and ye shall receive; knock, and it shall be opened unto you.'

They shall be caught up, and be where the eagles gather. They shall not be found wanting. Tell them that their Father has heard them. Their Father is ever gracious and ever loving to His children.

I am he who is only as great as the smallest particle of sand on the Earth and is only as low as the highest mountain top. I have known countless existences upon this beloved planet. To know now the sweet essence of the breeze and the cedars of Lebanon, the aspen of America; to feel the gentle waters caressing the many shores of the world; to know the harmony as the beautiful plant life of the planet responds to the minds of man.

On Earth the great kingdoms that would serve man: the mineral, the vegetable, the animal life— are in a state of chaos; because that which was created to be its master is not a master at all. The mineral life, the vegetable life, the animal life finds that its god, its master, is a drunken master who reels to and fro in his folly. That is why they now rebel against him. But on other worlds they respond and they caress their master, and the result is a vibrant life-giving essence that is beyond comprehension and my power to describe.

Has not the man often wished to go back to the security, the warmth of the mother? I say it is equally true of man for the Father. Man of Earth knows where he must go but he cannot always find the way. Therefore, the coming times directly ahead of you all point that way to Him; for that shall be your shibboleth of spirit.

I have spoken to you from out of the smallest of the creation on Earth and out of the largest: the small and the large being one in Him.

Peace to you from all Creation, and my peace to you.

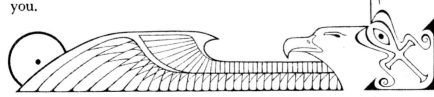

I have asked to speak with you again because for me it is the time of the great initiation and, in a smaller sense, of your great initiation to another plane of consciousness.

It was a time long ago that I was called to the Earth to perform a certain mission to the children of men. And now the time has come for me to return to Venus to be by her side as she enters the great initiation.

This day upon the Holy Sea of Galilee their armies clash by night. It is the beginning of the end and the end of the beginning, as it was prophesied of old, for today the long strife that has taken place in the 'unholy ' Holy Land has reached an apex, a culmination point—the armies of Egypt and Syria and the armies of Israel. This is a very significant happening, as my beloved Brother, Master Kuthumi, has told you many times.

This is the place to watch in the world, the place that is the spark which shall ignite the approach of Him whom we await; and do we not wait upon Him with exceeding patience and pleasure to dwell upon?

This is the lesson that we all must learn, not once but many times, in worlds of magnificent splendour as well as in worlds that are veiled and are dark in culture and development. How many times have we learned this lesson? And we will always continue to learn, for, take away curiosity and take away the thrill of living and seeking and man could not exist. There would not even be a creation. So we shall never reach the end of that road. We shall always seek. If it is not countries or lands and peoples, then it shall be worlds, or suns, or systems, or galaxies, or super-galaxies; and beyond that we shall know pleasure in the realms of light themselves, each one adding its own vibration and its own light.

One of the great laws is that in order to receive we must give, for, like the giant water-basin, it can receive the heavenly rains until it chokes and swells and runs over, but it must run over, giving of its abundance to the dry parched ground beneath it. If it does not, then it bursts and can contain no more. But if it does give of its abundance then, when the great rains come again from heaven, it will be replenished all the more and again can give as the hungry earth drinks in every drop and waits for the great water vessel to give of its abundance.

It was decreed long ago that I should come to Earth to assist our Elder Brother who rules this System, and to assist all our beloved brothers and sisters upon the Earth Planet. But I was at a certain time to return once again to my own Venus, the planet which has been given to me as my ward. Therefore I had to give whatever I had in abundance to my Earth children. Now that I have done that—and I say it without any feelings of egotism—and fulfilled this task, now shall I receive of the latter rains that will come. Only those vessels that have given receive of the latter rain. So ever is it a process in our development through many millennia. We give and we receive; but every time that we receive we receive more. The water vessel is not a stationary, permanent thing. It becomes ever larger, ever more shapely, ever more perfect in the eyes of the Father. From a crude clay vessel it becomes a vessel like unto a gem of finely cut crystal. Our entire Solar System is now coming into the great initiation, for it is true that we are now heading directly for the Super-sun which governs our Galaxy, around which countless island universes perpetually move and have existence. Our System is heading for the centre of this activity, and this increased rate of vibration will profoundly affect every-

thing in our System; whether it be mental, physical, or spiritual it will not escape the change in the new vibration of energy that is coming.

We are now on the border of this great initiation, we are heading closer and closer to its centre and fulfilment.

Therefore I would stand with Venus at this time. That is why Christ returns to the Earth: because always the great Master of a solar system incarnates and gives aid to the planet which is lowest in progression in that system, and also because He is the spirit of the Earth, which position He achieved in His incarnation as the teacher, Buddha. Buddha was for the Earth, but the Christ is for the System.

Let us take as an example two men. Both have committed the same error exactly in all its details. Each one has done the same thing. But can we condemn each man equally? No, we cannot condemn either man. But let us look into the cause of things. On the Earth man only looks to *effect* and never to *cause*. Once he looks into the heart of things he will find that it is the heart of the Father Himself; then from there all the rays of creation proceed out from Him. He will never find it by looking at the rays alone. He cannot trace it from effect to cause. It must be from cause to effect. So let us look not at the effect which is what each man has done but let us look at the *cause*.

Let us take one man. We find that he has done a certain thing through ignorance of the law. The other man had knowledge of the law. It is said in your world that ignorance of the law is no excuse, but in the Father's realm ignorance of law is an excuse. But once we have learned the law, if we falter and make error, then we are indeed in a different category than those who through ignorance perform the same thing. You see, the sin or error is not in stepping into the hole in the ground; the error is in stepping in it twice, once we know it is not the thing to do.

Therefore, I give this example to show you the condition that the Earth is in at the present time. The Earth has had many civilizations and, when one has gone to the bottomless pit, man rises in his cultural development and again builds a glorious civilization with great scientific and technical advance. But again the civilization drops to the bottomless pit. There is the error of the Earth, for on Venus there has never been a destruction of a civilization. On the planet you know as Mars it has occurred twice. But how many hundreds of times has it taken place on the Earth!

Man must learn to apply knowledge once he has attained it. You are now in the process of developing your physical forms. If you develop them and attain, yet do not apply what you have learned, you will soon lose what you have attained. In fact, you would perhaps be in worse condition than you were before you started.

So man on Earth must learn to apply the knowledge in constructive channels. Therefore, once we have asked (because the Father has said if we ask we shall receive)—once we have asked and have received, the law is we must apply what we have received, and then we must give what we have received.

I have received much during my mentoring on Earth, which now I go to give of myself to my own, my home and to my people. But the Earth shall always be close to my heart.

And now we enter this great period of initiation. The skies of Earth will become fantastic. Through many prophecies that have come to you from other

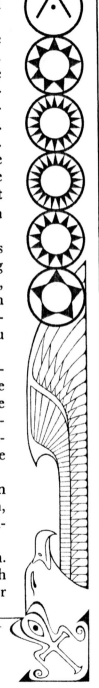

people working throughout the world, you feel that you have an insight into what shall take place; and yet I say verily that pen has not recorded nor voice uttered that which shall become a great sign and display in the skies of Earth, for the elements themselves will have control for a short period of time. There will be great rainstorms and floods. You have heard how it rained forty days and nights. That is nothing compared to what it will rain. Perhaps it would be forty months. The entire face of the Earth shall change. It will become unrecognizable.

Strange creatures shall appear from the depths of the oceans to the wonderment and bewilderment of man, creatures many times larger than the largest ocean liners. There shall be plagues and famines. Beasts and creatures unknown shall appear.

The Earth is about ready to become a 'sun,'—not like the Sun of your System,—but it shall be surrounded by a golden corona. It is stepping into a higher rate of vibration. It will become a 'sun'; but it is not known in your system of astronomy because it has never been viewed by your astronomers. You are going from a three dimensional to a fourth dimensional world. No longer will others be able to see you or your world. This must necessarily take place as you pass through the heart of the great cosmic cloud. And then shall the prophecies, as recorded by Joel and many of the others, come true: when the Sun shall turn blood red and the Moon shall be red as the ruby, and the day shall be gone and it shall be dark upon the Earth for a period of two weeks. There shall be much confusion. And the oxygen will be reduced upon the Earth for a short period, followed by periods of great moisture, baking heat and parched areas alternating with great moisture. Almost everything upon the face of the Earth will be destroyed.

When is this time coming? We are now in it. Each
day it grows in intensity. More of your craft that fly
in the air are coming down. Every day you hear of it.
More tornados! More floods! The Polar caps melt-
ing more each day! The water levels rising! Increas-
ing earthquakes!

The governments of the world are in panic, yet
they do not show it outwardly. Beneficial bacteria
upon the Earth which you depend upon are dying at
a rapid rate, so that you will be exposed more and
more to that which is detrimental to your physical
form.

All would end upon the Earth two years from today—all would be dead if it were not for the fact that
some will be able to raise their vibration to the new
level. But remember, as you see that which decays
and dies before your eyes, it is because all is being
made new. Rejoice that you see these things, for it is
your salvation which draweth nigh, and not your
doom.

And therefore you must tell your fellow-man that
the catastrophes will come, but that they are your
salvation. Rejoice! for the old passes away.

If man can release the *old*, then he shall glimpse a
more glorious *new*. Those who cannot release the old
will have to start again at the beginning. They shall
place their soul progression back several million years,
and once again will have to come up through various
forms of cave man through thousands of years, even
millions, until they develop to this very stage again.
And then they shall have the chance once again to
accept the new and, if they cannot accept the new,
they will go back once again millions of years.

This is not retrogression as it would appear. It is
retrogression in the physical, yet it is *progression* from
the standpoint of spiritual evolvement, for in the

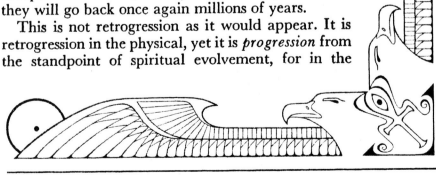

Father's realm there is no retrogression—only continual expanding grandeur. So that we might find ourselves worthy to pass through the great initiation! For whether a being or a man or a spirit or a soul entity commands a planet or a solar system or only his own little family, he never knows if he will stand the 'fire,' the test of fire of a great initiation.

Apply that which ye have learned and give gladly that which ye have received. As you travel and converse in the times ahead allotted for each one of us, think not what you shall take with you or what shall be in your purse or what you shall wear. Think not on these things because the Father will provide. Accept that and it shall be done unto you, for verily you have accepted a trust and a mission; and the Father will supply from His abundant storehouse unto you in that you serve well.

This is the time of giving and applying. And that is exactly what I myself go to do now. It is not the clarion call or the order which is given to you alone, but it is the order of the day as we enter into this new phase for the Planet Earth, and indeed our whole System.

Work, for the night cometh shortly when no man can work! Work for the night cometh! literally and figuratively. Man asks: 'We do not know what to believe. Some say catastrophe shall come upon us. They claim the end of the world is here. Others claim, "be not afraid; through our own scientific developments—we who are masters of the creation—can do this or that."' Man is seeking. His heart is hungrier than it has ever been because he feels the new vibrations.

Is it not true that a hungry man is even more hungry when he smells food? Even as Christ was tempted in the desert when He was fasting, is not a man who is fasting more susceptible to temptation of savoury morsels of food?

Man smells this food, this new vibration, and he becomes ever more hungry. It has whetted his appetite for things of Spirit. Therefore, when he is confused as he is and says, 'Brother, where shall I find the greatest meal which shall give me the most satisfaction for development of my spirit?' you shall say: 'Yes, those who say catastrophe comes are true; they speak with truth; but the *Earth will not end*. It shall become new, as it is written. It does not say the world will end. It says there shall be a "new heaven and a new earth," not a new Earth through the destruction of the old, but a *new* Earth—the old made new.'

So tell them the words with which the Elder Brother wishes you to feed His flock. It is the way of the Father. Catastrophe comes so that man might learn from the experience. But only the great and beautiful and good shall be inherited from it. Out of it mankind shall arise phœnix-like unto his own golden glory.

How often we look upon the Earth, knowing as we look upon each small and pitiful creation and creature, that here stands a god if he would only realize it and apply his godhead. For a true god sits not on a throne in inactivity while the masses come before him in adoration. That is not godhood as some on Earth would think, but godhood is enthronement, yes, but a god of action who enters the being of each one of his creation; fills them with life and majesty and grandeur.

God wishes man (man that He created) to rule over His celestial worlds. He wishes each man to take charge of His worlds. Recognize that each one of your fellow-men that passes you during the routine of the day—recognize him as a potential god. For

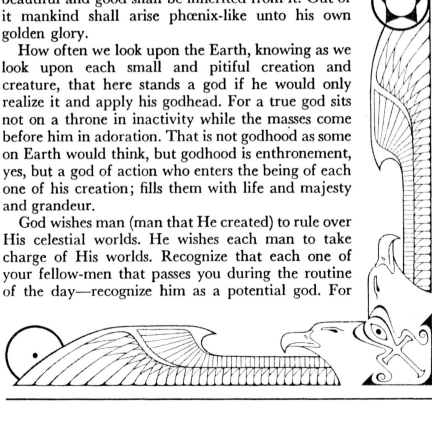

some day, each one, no matter whether they are in your institutions of correction, whether they have gone to your gas chambers, or to the hangman's noose, some day that soul will command a planet, and then a system and then a galaxy. We are all on the road to that legacy.

And the clarion call is: 'Come home Earth!' as I have said. 'Come home to the emptiness of our beings!'

When each man can feel the love and friendship from another man, then the lion shall lie down with the lamb, as it is written. For we are all part of one Eternal Mind and, to come back into that Mind, we must all unite our spirits.

Do not become weary from the routine of the day. Always keep the goal before you, not the eternal goal, for there is no eternal goal, but keep the goal of the moment which shall be an eternal goal, in a sense. Keep it before you ever shining like a great golden sun. Turn not your face from its radiance nor its warmth. Stay within it. Let it enshroud you in its warmth. Go where the Father doth lead. Do what the Father feels is best for you.

For this is the time that you have died countless times over, for which you have been crucified, whether you were a man or a man on a throne. Accept now your graduation, and prepare for the great initiation.

Archangel Michael

Ave! Ave! Realize that you are never alone, that it would be impossible for you to be alone. You are attached for eternity to the brotherhood of service.

The Golden Helmeted Ones surround the Earth ever more as we enter into the great initiation. We are plunging deeper into that which shall be our destruction and yet it shall be our salvation, even as He who went to the Cross of pain. It was His destruction; and yet it was His glorious Transfiguration.

May we be worthy of the Cross.

Joseph of Arimathea

Greetings in the light of the Cross. This is thy brother, Joseph.

I add my words to those of our teacher, Sanat Kumara, who now leaves us. And yet we have known of his spirit and his substance. Therefore he can never be completely gone from us.

But I wish to say to you: The Grail, remember The Grail. It is shining and glowing and beckoning even as it was to you long centuries ago when we held it within our hands. It is the symbol, the little clay Cup that symbolizes the Earth, that shall shortly be filled to overflowing, not with blood, but with the manna from the Father, the manna of true cosmic wisdom and understanding.

Beloved ones, receive, apply, and give freely. And soon we shall stand together, and we shall see The Grail returned to the Earth in the firmament. So be it!

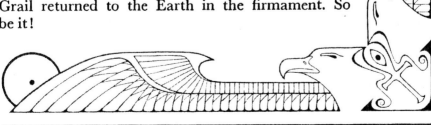

Archangel Uriel

Before the memory of man recounteth this tale, we beings known to mortal man as archangels were the only living thought in a certain limitless part of the Father's realm. He journeyed like the legions of Caesar, yet without weapon of stone or steel, but with Truth as a double-edged sword. Only Truth could exist in this vast ocean that you would fain call space. Yet it is not space. It is a breathing, living creature of such beauty and magnificence that if mortal man could view it he would cease to exist in form and in thought.

We were called out of the emanations of Deity because we were to know service and substance thereof. We came not at a trumpet's call but because in this void would appear shortly worlds and millions of the Father's creation. So-called angelic hosts of far away worlds, galaxies, systems and heavens, passed ever forward, in and out, cleansing and purifying with waves of violet haze and purple clouds.

Once we viewed a great spiralling ball of fire circling in its eliptical orbit, finally coming to rest in a certain position beyond the orb you know as the Sun, for this was an intruder; this was an intruding world that surrounded the Sun, because under the dazzling corona of this orb our world existed, not looking into blue of sky but looking into the gold of Sun, and the dazzling radiance of gold. There is more reality under the light of the Sun than there is in the blue of the sky in which the planetary worlds exist and know their movements.

We had known life on the Sun before the worlds came. Then the Earth—one of the newest members of the System—the child that was added, even as

Judas Iscariot was added as Twelve—was added as twelfth planet, the last of the worlds. They did not arrive according to their position from or to the Sun.

And after countless ages we watched this red ball of fire turn black as the fires diminished, and then brown, while the rains came; for millions of years it rained. At last the planet became green and brought forth all manner of flesh, flying creatures; and the creatures of the deep brought forth after their own kind; and the Earth was ready to receive the seed of man—angel-man. We have watched this procession down countless millions of years.

And now, out of the past, there is the sounding of a silver trumpet. When the Beloved Teacher, who is Lord in this Solar System, came to Earth, the heavenly hosts rejoiced, even as it is written they rejoiced on that night when He arrived. And above was the sign of the night: the Blue-White Star that came and embraced the Earth in its radiance and in its love from the angelic hosts afar.

O, man of Earth! you speak of the things of heaven, yet you understand not even the things of Earth. Indeed heaven is all about you! You have but to look up from your daily routines, from your daily misgivings and your waywardness, and your lusts and your greed, to realize that heaven is all about you in ever expanding grandeur.

And now, after all this time, for millions of years of rain, as we think on these things, the time that man has been on Earth is as but a moment. And yet again the rain shall come and purify. The rains that it is truly written of shall be the 'latter rain'—but first the winds. Going back through the stages of the planet in its earliest conception out of primordial and cosmic matter, and when the Earth has served its purpose, I

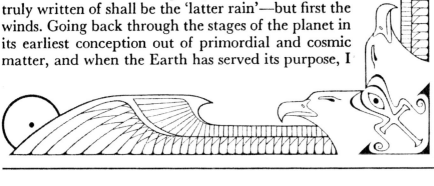

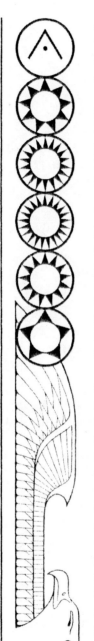

say verily it disintegrateth in thought. It returns to the elements from whence it came. And man moves on and on into greater lessons of spirit as he comes evermore to know himself.

Man looks to his many sorrows and does not understand; through love alone has the heart of a Caesar been touched and the trade stamp of truth been impressed upon his heart. Through the ages love has wrought its own miracles, and the hungry heart of mankind is now more open than ever before.

The hungry hearts of the world are crying for Truth, for they have starved on everything else. They have been given strict discipline, many religions, and materialistic science, but the human heart has not responded to these disciplines. And in that they have learned their great lesson, for now they know that only the emanations of Deity will satisfy their hunger, and they seek once again the sacred manna from heaven. I say verily the manna comes and it shall be seen of all men.

High in open heavens the host rusheth unto you now. It is truly written of them; they do not slumber nor sleep. 'The latchet of their shoes is not broken; their chariots swift as the whirlwinds; their swords sharp for the harvest; and the people roar against them like the roaring of many lions. Behold, there is darkness and sorrow upon the land.

So often one mortal becomes engrossed with the things of the day until all his energies are taken up and sapped of their strength by the futility of each day and its many blind alleys. Let us grasp at least a few moments of each day and see the vision that shall soon leave the kingdom of visions and fantasy and the kingdom of illusion, and shall come down and dwell among us; and it shall be real and we can feel of its great substance. For have we not served countless millennia in many lands, under many names, under many races? We have tasted of the fruits of many peoples of all flesh. Would that we could recount every single lifetime! If we could count and re-call each and every hand that has been laid upon our fevered brow in love, each stalwart arm of a young man that has supported us in our miseries and in our sorrows, the kind word of the loving neighbour or wife.

Let us remember the love that we have known through countless lives. These things are indelible. They exist forever in time. All of these things are still existing in time, for love perpetuates itself and never dies. Only hate expends itself in fury as the uncon-trolled vortex.

Dear ones, at this time we are sending you the ray and frequency of our beloved Master Teacher. For-get your surroundings. Lose yourself. Let your mind float in emptiness as though you are in the hand of the Creator.

I say that the Christ has never been more close to His followers, His servants, those beneath and below. Can you, with limited mortality, try to piece the pic-ture from the beginning when you came to Earth until now, or glimpse it as one great picture, and service? Listen quietly now for the still small voice.

It is my privilege to bring you these words of His. Listen for my voice in the sweetness of sleep as it wings its way toward you as the white dove of Re-demption. Listen! Watch, and wait! For the king-dom of which we spoke now cometh upon the Earth scene. Verily men have said, since we preached and ministered, the kingdom is at hand. Beloved, the kingdom is here now. Let us make ourselves a living part of its being.

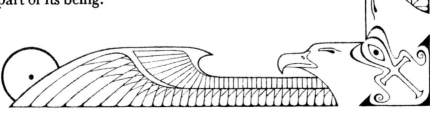

Archangel Michael

Ave sheoi! If you could but know the glory that exceedeth creative Light and the heavens rejoice. For, as the Golden Helmeted Ones sweep around the Earth and around again, we know that this is the time when to man, looking up at starlit night climbing the great rugged mountain, there shall come a day of great knowing to each heart.

The Day of the Great Telling that has been prophesied is now imminent in your affairs. You must now array yourself in full armour, as you have been tutored throughout all time. Do not fear the brilliance of the armour for it is your passport to higher realities. It is your shibboleth; it is your shield of the ages. Only by its effulgence shall you be known of man.

Spend more time in listening to the words of your Divine Father: one who shall speak in the plural and say, 'These are my beloved sons in whom I am well pleased.' The Four and Twenty Elders sit about the Throne waiting to receive you.

You are now coming to a time when it is of vast importance that you speak out so that many souls might be lifted in their final stage of development. Shortly all secrets shall be revealed in the light of the new day when nothing can stand that is hidden, nothing that is dark shall not be exposed to the Light. Some shall wither and decay; others shall spring forth in response to the new energy. All will be shown in its true form and state.

I cannot speak long for my light diminishes. My ray extended to you now retreats back to Source. But we speak not in riddles, nor do we speak in

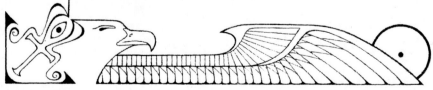

beauteous language merely to make a pretty speech. There is meaning there. Mark this well. Let all thy services be toward it alone.

Man now has attained the summit of his creation and perfection on Earth. It has served its age-long purpose, and now he stands atop a mountain. Man on Earth is enthroned as a god and does not even realize his own godhood!

Listen for the legions that march onward and ever onward, neither those of the Black Dragon, nor those of the black hordes of space. Listen for the Legions of the Light that penetrate your knowings.

There shall be a great blinding light and crash of thunder. Then man shall stand naked before his Creator and man will *know*, for all history has only been lived and written that man may *know*. Man has scaled the heights and depths of his experience on Earth to attain the godhood of knowing. And out of the rumblings and dust of the past he will hear his own voice.

Some day soon, after the Day of the Great Telling, a multitude shall witness and hear the voice that speaks to them, the voice that swells as a thousand angel voices, yet one, that says, "Come home, Earth! Come home. Come home!"

Archangel Raphael

Rama Eloi, Eloi Rama.

Remember, as the new vibrations come in as a tidal wave of spiritual Truth—and when I say tidal wave I mean the term literally and figuratively—that

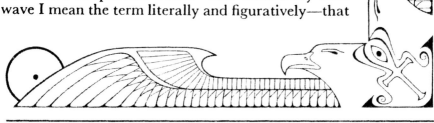

it will manifest on all planes: physical, mental, and spiritual—remember that the great winds of the Creator embrace you; the grass longs to play with your feet, the winds with your hair. By this I mean you shall stand unashamed as the flame before the altar that is He who is our Life.

The Golden Book is now open, the seal broken, never to be replaced; and in that Golden Book only a few names are written. The Earth is the Dark Red Star of Creation.

You can have no idea what shall be seen in the skies! Great spiritual manifestations! The entire world shall be on its knees! The rock shall fall on those who seek a refuge—those who have sought their brother's life—to the ever watching army of the golden horde, the host of the golden chariots and the golden wing. I add the double-edged golden sword, which is the Sword of Truth that emanates from the Father's mouth. It shall not fail in its judgment!

Archangel Michael

From this sphere of life is now emanating a golden mist that shall enclose your world even as from this sphere for countless millions of years your world has been enclosed in the golden radiance that has brought it heat and light, which is symbolic of the Father's Divine Love and Divine Wisdom—heat and light to warm man's physical being and to give him the flame of spiritual Life. For it is the affinity between this sphere and yours that makes for life and makes it possible for you to search for Truth.

Now from this sphere are gathering the Golden

Helmeted Ones who are now progressing toward your world: from all space the covenant of our Infinite Father, the convenant of the bow in the sky.

Shortly there shall be a bow that has never been seen before in the sky of Earth, a bow of magnificent colour, from which emanates musical sounds that shall come to the ear of all men, and they shall know a calling; they shall know a love; they shall know a duty. From this bow of beauty, this bow of duty that calls to its own, it shall first appear as a great violet radiance over the entire world: the Golden Helmeted Ones from our sphere who have never come so close to Earth before. Only in ages past have they appeared to Earth in a very few cases on very special errands for the Infinite Father. And they were given the title of Archangels, the spiritual messengers who were above the angels or the messengers, the mentors of the messengers.

Now they come for this final gathering of the chariots of gold when they shall gather to subdue the last remains of the darkness of Earth; for over the entire world a golden glow shall manifest itself, and, when it lifts, those who remain will know truly they are their brother's keeper.

This is our part of the mission, for it will not be long when this sphere itself is no longer of use. And this is always the work of those who live in the very centre of their solar system, and under the golden corona of light. Man has always looked to this great orb for his very life, and rightly so that he should.

O, man of Earth! awaken to these new chords that are not lost chords. Indeed, they have never been lost! Always they have remained—the five-stringed lute that man of Earth would play and yet not under-

stand the music thereof.

Now there is a new chord, a note that is real—not weird—but full of zeal for the men of Earth who would themselves apply feathers and wax to develop wings that they might fly up to the great Sun Body, for in this legend of the youth who would fly to the Sun—and yet his wings were melted—there lies a truth that man wished to fly to this great body which gave him life, for he believed that by being encompassed within it he would find himself and the eternal mystery of mysteries. For the ancient peoples of your world did not believe that this body was one of great flames and heat; they understood its true meaning as the centre and life of this System.

Now this body is in great age, as celestial bodies do age. It has existed for fifteen hundred billion years. Now it shall die, announcing its end to the far corners of the Universe as a great exploding star. But the end is a beginning, for it has served us well and we march on: Humanity of this System marches on to other portions of the Father's realm.

Yet this orb shall not end until the Millennium has passed, when once again the forces of darkness are released. Then shall the end come and this System disintegrateth in thought. For it is only thought— since all celestial bodies, whether star or world, are only the forms in which our Father's Words are formed. They are His Words that were spoken in the beginning that there should be Light and there should be substance. They are His Words, and some shall disintegrate in thought—that which was only thought in the beginning.

Some day, in the not too distant future, you shall look upon a great purple plain ahead, a golden light that draws you to it by its heat and warmth. Imagine what awaits those of Earth who have proved themselves to be His children! They shall not want for Truth. For many centuries our Father has heard the words of the sincere on Earth: 'Our Father, thy will be done on Earth as it is in heaven.' This prayer is now to be answered.

It *shall* be on Earth as it is in heaven. Man shall no longer want for anything. He shall shortly take his place as a true son of God, for did not the Master, Jesus the Christ, say: 'Know ye not that *ye* are gods?' Know this and accept the sceptre and orb of your godhood, not that you would exalt yourselves above your fellow-men, but that you accept the gift that the Father has always kept waiting for His children who would but see the Light.

And you shall set foot on plains of unbelievable grandeur—you and the others of Earth who are the Harvest which the angels now come to reap. This Harvest shall be gathered tenderly and bound together and stacked in the fields awaiting the proper light that has an affinity with their light. And then they shall vanish from the Earth. In a twinkling they shall be gone. Then they shall come into a great natural amphitheatre while all the angels, as it is written in your Holy Scriptures—the Holy Scriptures that were written on command and authority of the Light from this sphere—shall sing before His Throne. It is truly written and this shall be.

And when the singing takes place it is singing that has never been heard on Earth, for it is a mingling of the souls of all those who partake of this fellowship. Animals and birds partake in this vibrational singing of the spheres. And you shall see before your eyes a fantasia of beauty and colour and sound and harmony mingling together in worship to the Light that is the I AM.

And you shall see opening up before you beautiful

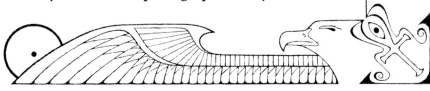

flowers and tree and vines, and they sway to and fro in response to your singing, and open their petals and faces, straining upward, turning to look at the Sun. All the Father's Creation shall respond together for, as we see you from this sphere, you are not countries or nations or individuals or animals or slaves or free, *you* are *one* being, the being that is Earth. You are one MAN, a man with many wounds, who shall soon be free and soothed of his wounds.

Even as you go about your mundane activities of the day, search the deepest part of your heart. Realize with joy that this is the time we have been waiting for. Let your fellow-man know the Master soon shall place His foot upon Earth again. This is the time when all men can rejoice. The bells of heaven are ringing! The trumpets are sounding!

Archangel Gabriel

They do not mean what is written. 'Father, Father, why hast thou forsaken me?' Why should the Master, who vowed constantly the Aton—the One God— why should He in desperation finally doubt the Father and say, 'Why hast thou forsaken me?' These are words of cowards, of those who have not fulfilled their mission, not the words of The Christ. These have been misinterpreted, for they are not in the Aramaic language of the time. They are in the most ancient Solar or Mother Tongue which, of course, the Master would revert to at that time. The words are not 'sabachthani'; they are spelled with a 'z'— 'zbacthani': z-b-a-c-t-h-a-n-i. 'Eli, Eli, lama zbac-thani' means: 'Those who defame me shall keep open my wounds'—'those who defame me shall keep open my wounds.' 'Eli, Eli, lama zbacthani.' 'Father, unto thee I commend my spirit; it is finished.' The great war machines of the world are now massing together. In the Holy Land we see the beginning of the end for Earth. Once again Egypt and Israel. Is it not significant? And it shall grow and grow. The greatest battle that has ever been seen shall take place, not only among those who fight their fellow-men but also amongst the elements. The Earth itself shall find a battlefield. The forces of Nature shall be unleashed because of man's wrong thinking and do-ing, as he has worshipped in word and not deed, and has not served the Master.

What a great time it was when the heralds of heaven called forth the announcement that this night 'Peace on Earth' for He—He who was Buddha, He who was the Light of Asia, the 'Light of the World' manifested in the humble surroundings that night.

I was Gabriel of the Sun, as my Brothers, but since that time I have been Gabriel of the Star Craft until this work is completed.

The armies shall be stopped by a great natural cataclysm. The weapons shall melt in their hands. They will find finally that the Earth has reached the place where the vibrations no longer will tolerate an act of wanton murder on the part of its inhabitants. For centuries man has spilled blood upon the Earth over and over again. Not one moment of one day has passed without a man's blood being spilled upon the Earth. Now the vibration refuses to kill.

It will not be an act of the Father, nor an act of superior military equipment. It will be man's own thinking rebounding upon him. By his thinking over many thousands of years the vibration has been created. Finally, in the great war when man raises

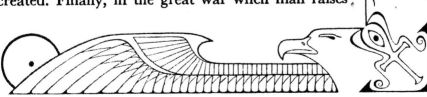

his weapons against his fellow-man, they will not function in the new vibration. Anything that will cause destruction will melt. If a man utters a destructive word, he will disintegrate. Anything negative will vanish.

All government and authority must collapse, as it is written, before He returns. We do not preach sedition; neither tyranny nor the acts of traitors. We preach Jesus the Christ!

How can this nation of the United States of America or any nation on the Earth claim that it is following the Master as it builds greater forces of destruction, greater ways of killing fellow-men. Your leaders claim it is a truth that the more power they have the more peace we shall enjoy. You do not win peace by placing a gun in a man's back. What kind of a peace is this but the peace of idiots and fools and of those who serve Satan.

When the Master was Buddha He uttered the great truth: 'How and when will hate cease if it is met with more hate?'

Your country is not Christian! It is not following the Master Jesus. If it was it would lay down arms and destroy all its atomic weapons. It would have no weapons of destruction or protection. It would rely on Him alone to protect them. He is the only protection. Therefore, this country which was prepared to lead the world now must go down with that world, as it was written.

All nations shall collapse utterly and completely upon the face of your Earth! And then the new government, with Christ as King and the house of David once again shall reign supreme.

There shall be those things, those portents and signs, the like of which the world has never before seen. The seas shall rage! The monsters of another age shall roam the land. The great creatures that once lived, weighing many, many tons, shall again roam the streets. Famine shall appear. Great pestilence of locusts. The seas shall give up monsters that the Earth thought long dead and they shall crawl on the shores.

And all these things soon; but have we not prepared? Are we not made for this time knowing that out of it shall come the greatest good of all for all men everywhere as they progress in ever expanding grandeur up, and up, until they reach the heart of God. And when they reach the heart of God, there shall be other hearts to ascend. Truly it is said, *'Quo vadis Domine?'*—'Whither goest thou, Lord?' We shall always say, 'Whither goest thou, Lord?' as He receives every promise in His progression. And when we become lords and gods, and rulers of universes even, He shall still be the Lord and we shall yet be called His friends.

I speak now of world government, with your permission. Atlantis shall again have a Poseid, and Lemuria a Zorai. The Inca shall have their Inca, and Egypt a Pharaoh. In Egypt, one of the great centres of world government, as a new Pharaoh starts a new dynasty, it shall be known in millennia to come by historians as The Golden Dynasty. The great seven colonies of the Motherland are returning, as well as the Motherland. The Brotherhood at Lake Titicaca will return the great Golden Sun Disc to the Temple of the Sun.

The new government of the world shall be based on the ancient government of the Sun, which modern scientists do not understand. It was not the worship of the Sun itself. It was the purest form: the adoration of Aton—the at-one-ment that the Master created by the giving of His blood that poured from

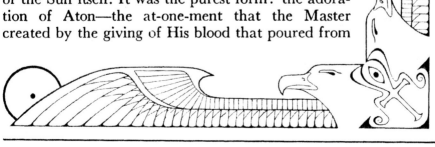

His side on Golgotha. It established the vibration in the Earth that made forever the eternal ray from the Earth to the Father, a ray that will not end. This was the purpose and meaning of His death on Calvary.

Would the Great Creator of all send His Son to die in despair and failure on the Cross? This implies that the Creator admitted defeat. He makes no errors! We make error. Jesus came to the Earth to live, not to die! Tell that to your churches. They say, 'Jesus came to die so that all men might be saved by the shedding of His blood.' He did not come to die. If He came to die why would the Father have sent Him in the first place? They imply in their fundamental and narrow teachings that Jesus came to teach men, but they rejected the truth. Therefore God, His Father, had no alternative but to place His Son on the Cross so that through the shedding of His precious blood all men might be saved and secure for themselves an everlasting and eternal free passage and quick ticket to paradise. This is the mouthing of Amun! It is not the teachings of our heavenly Father.

Jesus did not come to die primarily. He is not the dead Christ. Their entire gospel is based on the fact that Jesus died for them. He lived for them, dear ones; He did not *die* for them! We must follow His teachings, His words, His life. Instead they are living in the shadow of His death. They do not *live* His teachings, and they call themselves Christian nations. They are not Christian. They follow the Dark One.

Their munitions factories, their secret smoke-filled chambers are not the chambers where the Christ would come. That is why this farce, this United Nations, shall collapse. On the surface it is the sheep's clothing, but inside it is a ravening beast. It is not based truly on the life of the Master. If they would forget about His death and how it secured them an easy way into heaven, they could solve the world situation.

But they have been given their chance. Now it is too late. The sickle is being thrust into the field, and the fire set to the altar that shall determine what is chaff and what is pure gem. The stubble shall be burned; only the gems shall remain.

For the next several decades the Earth shall be wrapped in chaos of the very worst kind. She shall switch her axis, not once but three times. Dante with his *Inferno* could not picture such tragedy! I am not a prophet of gloom; I am a prophet of the facts. Because it is tragic, yes, but it is more tragic to see this continue. The quicker it is eliminated the quicker the new vibrations are established and the better for all men. Even those who perish shall be released to move on and learn where they must learn.

The law is that there is no retrogression, only progression. There are on Earth at this time only a few who can progress in this environment. All others shall vanish in one way or another.

At this moment a comet heads for the Earth that is bigger than the Earth, eleven times. It comes from the region of Vega. It is foretold in the *Book of John* that a great stone shall hit the Earth as the Earth passes through the tail of this comet.

The government of the Earth, the very heart and headquarters of it, shall not be on the Earth. There will be twelve who will sit as representatives in the council of Earth who rule as Pharaoh, Inca, Zorai, and Poseid, and the others. But He who rules the Earth as His footstool shall not then be on the Earth. And I speak not in riddles, although Gabriel is known to speak in riddles. It is only a riddle to those of little understanding. But the real government of

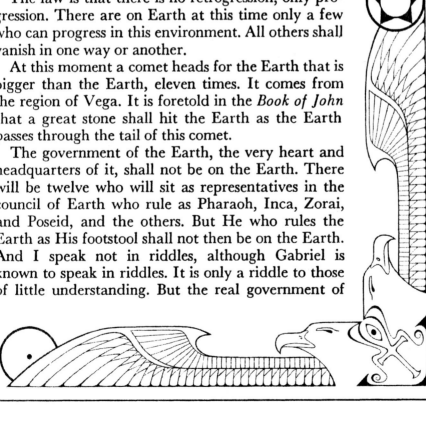

the Earth shall be from another Star, yet not a Star of millions of miles of distance, but one that becomes the Earth and it attached to it, and shall be known as Zabeka Musor, a School of Life.

Archangel Michael

For a moment, if you will, go back with me to a remote age of antiquity, far greater than we could comprehend in terms of Earth years, and picture in your mind a great spiralling mass of violet-blue flame rising upward leading man on to ever-expanding grandeur in the Universe of our Father.

Remember what Jesus has said: 'I know of no other Great Spirit beyond the Father. He is the Ancient of Days. I know, beloved ones, of no other beyond Him, yet I know that there are others beyond Him. I believe they exist.'

What is this hierarchy of Gods, of Creators, in the Omniverse? I wish to emphasize this so that you may understand the terminology. It is true, as some of you have suggested, God the Father is the Father that Jesus speaks of. He is a Creator-God, the Creator-God of all ancient mythology and legend. He is the God—God the Father—Thought Incarnate on the Star Sun Sirius. But there are Gods beyond Him of magnificence beyond comprehension.

There are worlds in space where man is nothing but ever-changing colour and hue, worlds of fantastic iridescence and glowing beauty, where one form mingles with the other, always one, always changing. There are worlds where man becomes only a tone as a tinkling bell, where life is only a kaleidoscope of nature, worlds that we cannot even begin to comprehend, that would make God the Father—Thought Incarnate on Sirius—appear as a grain of sand on a lonely beach.

Yet above all of this the Omniverse itself is the ALL, the PERFECT ONE, the INFINITE FATHER, the ALL CREATOR, the SELF CREATED ONE, and we call HIM in our Order simply EVERNESS.

What is behind this plan now unfolding upon the Earth? There is a greater plan beyond, even beyond the migration from this Solar System, as we gave you before, and the answer to that is that we are being called from out of the depths of night in space to serve those who cry out to us.

What is the purpose of the schoolroom of Earth? What means all the tears, sorrow, death, misery, anguish? For personal development, yes, but what else? What is the·grander plan? Only that a world will become a cinder through an atomic war? No! The lesson to be learned is that Spirit may come to know Itself, that man might be freed from the blight of the great adultery.

One day on your Earth shall come a blinding flash of light. All the old shall pass away, burned as chaff on the altar of truth. Only the 'gems' will remain, the 'gems' that can withstand the Eternal Flame.

The Earth is a school for gods. Man—the small Harvest of man upon the Earth—man who has lost the vestiges of the human—there are those on Earth today. It is written, not that the Harvest is great; or is it? Yes, it is written thus: and the labourers few. The Harvest is great according to the labourers, but from the total of the Earth's population, the Harvest is small.

It has taken millions of years since man has been upon the Earth to bring about this one small con-

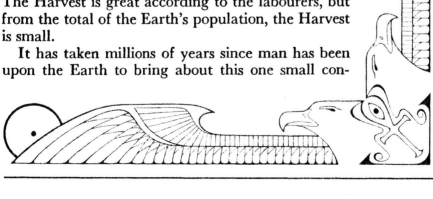

centrated drop of life to evolve in the crucible of time.

The Earth is a classroom for godhood—not Mars, nor Venus, nor Jupiter, nor magnificent Saturn, nor spiritual Neptune, Pluto nor Mercury, nor even the Sun and its many bodies. The lotus rises from the slime of earth. And now there is a single bloom. The Father looks down from blue of sky and gold of Sun and sees a single pure lotus opening from the slime, and shortly He reaches down to pluck it and to take it home again.

Therefore you and your fellow-men everywhere are being conditioned for Great Transmutation. And then we march on to other universes and worlds that call for our help. When man achieves his graduation day and wins his godhood, the work begins. Over countless millions of years man has risen from animal to become angel again! Think of the lives and the intrigues, the battles, and the loves that have gone to produce one drop of the eternal elixir!

Let us lose ourselves in this ever expanding army, a living thing that shall one great dawn shine forth as a golden glow over all the Earth. Those that run to the rocks will find no shelter. No bomb-proof shelter will give adequate safety. No cavern is deep enough, no mountain top high enough, for this is the day of the Great Transmutation when all elements shall be changed. Not only are you being prepared for other atmospheres, but you are now changing dimensions. You are leaving the world, the kingdom of the third dimension. You are entering the dimension of *understanding*. Accept that which the Father has for you.

The physical, as it is developed, is only to serve for a brief time. Work as one, for even though you know it not, you stand at this moment before the Throne of God the Father.

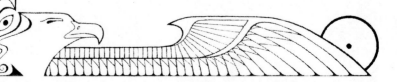

Some day we shall together look back upon our Solar System and see it explode like a star in the farthest corner of the Father's realm, because when it has served its purpose it disintegrateth in thought.

In truth we are an army. There are corners of the Omniverse where there is no light, only darkness, and even an army can only appear as a small pinpoint of candlelight. But remember the great truth that no matter how vast the darkness, no matter how vast the night, one small candle flame holds back that great darkness. In its insignificance it is invincible because it is light.

Then, as a tiny candle flame, we shall burst forth into an area that has never before known light and shall bring, even as the workers brought to ancient Egypt, the light, through Akhnaton. The people had never seen it before. Some it blinded, for it was too bright. They did not, as today, understand because of its blinding light. It was a thing to be shunned, to fear. And many fell back into the comfort of darkness.

Man is afraid of dark? We say, no; this is not true! Man is afraid of light. He wishes once again to be in the darkness of the womb where there is no light, for there alone he feels safety, warmth, and life. It takes courage to go into the light—not the dark.

Archangel Gabriel

There have been confusions of the mind for the Earth Planet. Although those of Earth call Mars the god of war, Saturn the god of gloom, Neptune the god of mystery, Pluto the god of Hades, no!—those

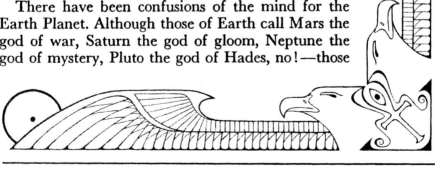

are the attributes of the Red Star, the Earth: gloom, despair, death, war! This planet has been in the grasp, and is in the grasp, of the black hordes from a distant galaxy, known to those of the Oriental world as the order of the Black Dragons, now incarnate on the Earth in Communism and all totalitarian movements. They sit on the thrones of Earth. Verily I say, they sit on all the thrones of Earth.

This a woman knew that night above Bethlehem. She knew that there were the workers already upon Earth who were performing the task that they had come for—the Lesser Avatars who came to do this work, not merely at this time but who had come countless millennia before. They had served with this Teacher, whether He was Buddha, Zoroaster, Melchizedek, Shem, and others. But she knew that her duty would be fulfilled for the first and the last incarnation upon that Red Star when He would come again for the day, Michael's day of the Great Transmutation.

The black hordes now are suffering the death throes of the Dragon, and in the death throes of a beast many will perish; but finally, the beast goes down to defeat. The martyrs of God shall rejoice!

Jesus said: 'Look what they have done to the Master! If this is so, what will they do to the servants?' Your heart and soul, your work and hand must touch the brow of those who are constantly turning their eyes upward, looking for that cloud that shall come. Your presence will still their souls; one day you shall walk by their sides rejoicing and singing, as it is truly written: 'The fields and all the trees shall clap their hands with joy,' for we go out in peace as we are taken up in the hand, as we gather where the eagles gather and find that once again we are in His hand.

If man on Earth only understood that each and every soul is precious in His sight, no matter how degraded. All shall eventually rise at the sound of a calling and move on as one. Man is destined to be placed upon the throne of the Omniverse to survey all stars, planets, suns, worlds, which are HIS thoughts in action.

There is no ultimate. There is only living—but first serving.

Brother philip

What you are now doing is preparing for post-catastrophe. It is already too late to do anything about catastrophe or pre-catastrophe. Many feel that the Space Visitors will come and provide all. I can assure you they will not. They will only assist.

Living will have to be by the conventional means and ways of Earth. That will be for a short period, and in quick order a great Utopian civilization will then arise from the Earth phoenix-like.

But we find that many are not yet ready. They cannot give up the comforts and those things to which they have been accustomed, and yet, after the catastrophes start these luxuries and comforts will have no purpose whatsoever. How can they wash their clothing in these machines, without electricity? How can they run their homes at all? They will have to go out in the back yard and use the barbeque pit to cook food. The electric stove will not work. They cannot light a fire in it. The gas will not work. They will have to move out of their homes to live at all: back to the caves.

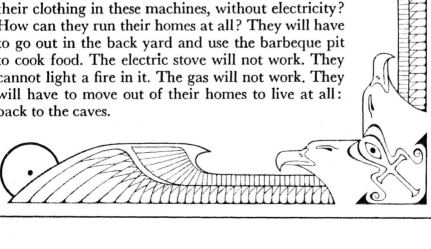

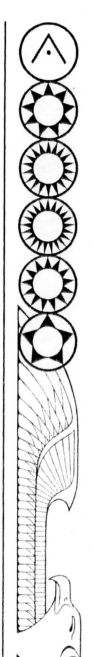

Man on Earth must not revert this time to savagery as he has done in the past. That is one of the great purposes of the coming of the Space People—to avert this catastrophe—because the Remnant, unless assisted, will go back to the caves. They have no other choice.

And many will die because they will not be as skilled in manufacturing weapons to secure food and other necessities as their cave ancestors were. They will not be adapted physically nor have the strength and endurance to live.

I can tell you now without pessimism that the next seventy years will be such. The New Age will not be here in a moment with crystal cities spread throughout the Earth. It cannot be done in a second. It will mean about seventy years of hard work building an earth, totally destroyed, into a New Age after the coming of Jesus once again. He will not wave a magic wand and all will follow the sheep and graze in the pastures as the Master takes them by the hand to lead them into Utopian fields. This will not be. It will be work and more work in developing the new world.

Then for roughly the same period man shall be a student, learning from his fellow-men on Earth who are more advanced than he. He shall be tutored by his Brothers from outer space, especially the young men interested in the scientific and electronic aspect, while other jobs will be more sociological and historical to show man the past and the true nature of past civilizations and its significance to the present, and to teach him the true history of the world, while the Space Visitors will be teaching him how to build the new world, the new science. All must be made new. The Truth must be revealed; in order to develop a new-world man, who will be hungry for that which is true.

Yet seventy years is a short time. At the end of it the Earth will be cleansed and purified, and then there *shall* be the crystal cities and there *shall* be space travel. But when that takes place man will find that he has joined the Interplanetary Brotherhood through his own efforts and has earned his chair on the Council of the Nations' Planets, only to discover and learn the secret of why the Space People have come to the Earth. It has been said many times for many reasons: because of our atomic experiments, because of this or that. All these things are true, yes, but also there seems to be a paradox.

The Space People themselves state that by Universal Law they cannot interfere with man's progression on the Earth. Is that not true? Yet they are interfering, are they not? And is it true that they are here out of love for their fellow-man? No! Because they would have put in a mass appearance centuries ago if it was purely for love. Do they love less or did they love less then than now? No! Somewhere there seems to be something missing—the key to the entire situation. Then why do they interfere now? What is the real reason? The answer as you have been told is that the eventual evacuation of this Solar System will become imperative because of the intense cosmic bombardment and harmful rays ensuing. This System will be absorbed into the development of a new embryonic sun and become a part of it, and utilized in its development. We are now swirling into that sun like a leaf in a whirlpool.

After man wins his seat on the Council he shall find he has only achieved it to work with his other brothers of space, representing the various worlds and solar systems, to assist in a great evacuation. And at that time the remnants of all the worlds who deserve it, through proper living and past lives, will

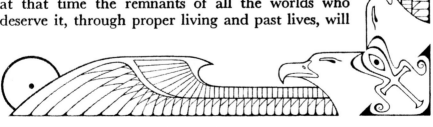

go on this great journey.

Man shall take a journey to the unknown, a vast part of interstellar space that has never been explored by man before, a space which has only been rumoured in legend of the most ancient planets, and known as The Void of Eternal Light. The possibilities and the new existence that the mind of man shall find here defies explanation, an entirely new development in the mind of man when he shall again have restored to him the power of Creative Thought, where he shall learn to begin the creation of worlds.

The thought is staggering and it shall be some time in coming. Great armadas will take man on this journey, and he shall discover and spend time studying many worlds before reaching this space. The journey shall take a long time to complete.

But, after man has achieved and brought the Earth back into the Brotherhood, then he will sit down to begin to plot this journey with his fellows of other worlds. He will be given the secret why the Space People had to come when they did in order that the Earth might be raised quickly because they could not await for the appointed time. Things had speeded up to such a degree that they could not wait for the Earth to come into its own gradually through karmic lesson. Interference was essential. Therefore, because of their motive, the karma that they must bear for their interference will be very light. It will balance itself. . . .

Master Kuthumi

Greetings in the Wisdom of the Ages. Several things now bear watching: Of prime importance is

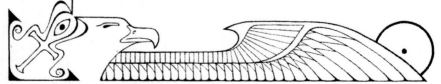

this so-called peace between Israel and Egypt; it is to be watched because it is not permanent. Even now the seeds are being sown and the war is raging. This peace is on the surface only.

This day (April 23, 1956) has been a momentous day for the people of Earth, although it will not be recognized as such for several decades. But this day (and you will hear of it shortly), on Earth, scientists have created life. For a long time they have worked on this. They no longer need roosters to produce chickens; and they have done this with frogs. It has taken place for some time. But today, by the mixing of certain chemical elements they have produced virus. They have created it themselves. The next step will be to create single cell organisms and keep them sustained. That is the problem—to keep them alive once they are created. And it was known in our writings that when this happened it would be another sign of the times.

But so startling shall be the developments of the New Age after catastrophe that in the short seventy-year span man will have gone ahead in his development—in seventy years he will have spanned one hundred thousand years. He will create from Light. For instance, a man falls under a train. Both limbs are severed from the body. He can—if there is not too much loss of blood and the physical can be kept alive until he is brought into the area of apparatus (I will not say hospital because that implies other things)—through light energy be restored, even to complete organs and brain. And this is only the beginning.

The new children being born are of a different order. They are from an area in space that now needs the Violet Ray experience. They will incarnate upon the Earth.

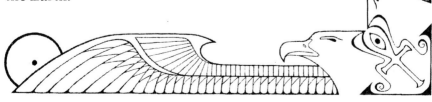

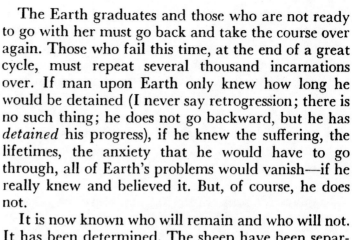

The Earth graduates and those who are not ready to go with her must go back and take the course over again. Those who fail this time, at the end of a great cycle, must repeat several thousand incarnations over. If man upon Earth only knew how long he would be detained (I never say retrogression; there is no such thing; he does not go backward, but he has *detained* his progress), if he knew the suffering, the lifetimes, the anxiety that he would have to go through, all of Earth's problems would vanish—if he really knew and believed it. But, of course, he does not.

It is now known who will remain and who will not. It has been determined. The sheep have been separated from the goats, the black from the white, the wheat from the tares. The survey is completed. It is known into which camp each man will go.

Following the seventy years, the Millennium begins in full, and then the period of reconstruction is over and all is made new, as it is written. All the old forms have been removed. The new Truth, whether it be history or whatever field it may be, has been installed.

For one thousand years the rule of The Christ upon the Earth, and then we shall have no need of Earth. During the Millennium period man will have reached great heights. Those who deserve to remain and can then move on with the others in space to the new area of Light of which the Teachers have spoken, for by then the Sun of our System will no longer support the planets. Our System is doomed to be absorbed into a new embryonic sun. It is now rushing thousands of miles per second toward its doom like a moth to a candle flame. When all is made new in the twinkling of an eye, as it is written in your prophecies, men feel that all will be paradise in one moment. I say it cannot be done. But the Earth will change its

time scale. Actually, there is a change going on in your dimension and in your time field. There will be a short rest period which will seem to you as ten years. In one important hour you may gain the experience of a lifetime.

If your fellow-men say to you: 'Do you think there will be an atomic war?' ask them if they believe in prophecy, that has been written in the Holy Bible and elsewhere. If they say, 'Yes,' then say: 'You have answered your own question,' because it is very plainly written in the prophecies what shall take place. The Master said: 'Those who can see and hear.' There are very few who really see and hear. Those who refuse to see are like the drunkard in the burning saloon who refuses to believe the party's over. The world is still dining and wining itself at the hour of doom. In fact the music is louder and the drinks stronger in order to drown the sound of the end of the Age. And it was prophesied that man would do this when disaster came upon him.

From the overall picture it is a lesson learned only, making them stronger in spirit. But to my words I add to those of my Brother Sanat Kumara, that the greatest conflict the world has ever seen or dreamed of will take place before we can begin the period of reconstruction.

Certain world leaders, the real world leaders, are now preparing for that which has been written and prophesied. While they have been giving the warning from our Brothers from space, they have disregarded it. They go on planning destruction. They know that increased atomic experimentation continues to melt the Polar ice caps, but they are not attempting to stop. The world is in the hands of little, mad men. They are literally mad. But they *shall* be removed shortly. The Earth will be swept clean of them as

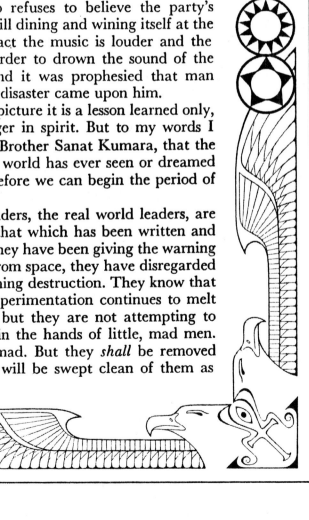

though a loathsome infection has been swept away. It seems to be a world of madness with no purpose, but in the total picture the madness was of so terrible a nature that those souls who came through it could not be anything but greater for it. The test of fire tempered them beyond all other experiences. From worlds in space there are souls who are actually crying to be born upon the Earth. Why should they renounce their celestial abodes for so violent and loathsome a world? Because here alone can they achieve the lessons of spirit that such an evil world can give. Yet it is a beautiful planet from the standpoint of its natural creation, far more beautiful than its neighbours. Mars is a desolate, aged world, not particularly beautiful. It does not have the scenes that you have.

It is man, crawling like vermin upon the surface of the Earth who has contaminated and destroyed it wherever he goes. Man always destroys. And this applies to the other planets as well because, while they have progressed beyond man on Earth, they are still far from perfect. They make many errors. Just as you would seem perfect to a savage, yet you know you are not. Thus do the men of other worlds appear to us, but they are far from perfect and they know it.

The Earth, because of this, is able in a short space of time to give qualities to Spirit that would take many, many lifetimes on other worlds to achieve. In fact, perhaps they could never achieve that particular experience.

The Earth is a classroom for gods, but a strange classroom indeed! Some of the people of the more magnificent worlds are actually envious—if they can be envious (but that is the closest word I can think to explain it)—because they know that on Earth, if you can combat such negativity you have to be a powerful spirit.

I am not complimenting the people of Earth, but those who have undergone lifetime upon lifetime and still come back. There is no law that says we have ever to come back; we do it of our own choosing because we know that only here will we learn the lessons. We could stay in eternal paradise. We do not have to return to physical life. After all, we have all eternity to do it. Yet remember that everything, negative and positive, is the Father. Without the negativity He would not have existence. Therefore He is both 'evil' and 'good,' positive and negative, Mother-Father God.

Master Kuthumi

We have said many times that this is the time for action. Philip has called me tonight to speak to you on matters of great importance. The forces are now aligning even more closely, as you have felt. The message that I bring you is a message of false prophets. Who they are and how we may know and recognize them.

You will find in certain communications it is stated that there are some who have no spark of divinity left in them. This is a falsity. There is no creature in the universe, no matter how evil or degraded that does not possess one tiny spark of divinity. Without this divinity it could not exist.

The second falsity is that such beings are annihilated by Divine decree. Nothing is ever annihilated by Divine decree. The great flood that destroyed the abominations of Earth was a Divine decree, yes, but why was it? It had been made so before by the creatures themselves. A certain course of action had

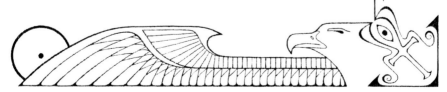

to be taken. But the implication is that they are annihilated from memory, annihilated as individuals. I tell you that even our Divine Father cannot annihilate you as an individual! Once He put His immutable laws into effect even He could not change them.

You may have wondered at this confusion. At times it sounds good; it fits. At others it is completely out of line. The reason is obvious. When the receiver is perking high and mighty it is tuned up and the individual strikes a higher level; otherwise the astral comes through. The only thing wrong with them is they are astrals and therefore they are not as aware as most mortals. You might as well go down the street and ask anyone you pass for advice. That does not mean that they are evil. There is nothing wrong with astrals. There are many wonderful beings who are astrals, true, but just being an astral does not make them anything special. You have to know what they were before they were an astral. You might like to talk to Gandhi if he is an astral, but I don't think that Dillinger would give you much. Why is it that the world suffers under the misconception that as soon as they pass over they have wings and the knowledge of Solomon, that because of their recent death they can impart great wisdom?

The astral forces are helping too. There are many great beings who are assisting both space men and yourselves. They are acting as emissaries, doing what work they can. Some of them perform fine services on the battlefields, on the streets, and in the offices, each acting as mentors and guides to the people of the world. After all, we have all been astrals many times. We have been astrals as many times as we have been mortals in that sense. I do not imply that everything astral is negative.

But you may question those who call others black

sheep. Is it possible that they themselves are the black sheep? For it is written that the forces of darkness will come as angels of light, especially in this time that has been prophesied.

What has come through under the Nostradamus forces is true. When the Master appears He will be called Satan, as He was called a drunkard and a whoremonger when He was on the Earth, but this did not change His duty nor His mission. Therefore, those now who are calling other people's material 'phony,' astral impressed, they are the ones to watch out for, because we need not point a finger at anyone if we have Truth. A false prophet will do that, and you can tell this to your people: beware of the false prophets because they came in sheep's clothing and, unfortunately, some actually think they are working for the forces of Light. Poor misguided souls! They are aiding the forces of anti-Christ in stirring up dissension. Those who are working with the Christ Light need prove nothing. Their own work is their calling card. 'By their works ye shall know them; by their fruits ye shall know them.' Is that not true? You do not have to call from the housetops to tell them who you are.

Tell this to your people: The space people are beings, three dimensional like ourselves. They are not 'spooks.' There are beings of other dimensions that are working with the Space Confederation but they are not coming into your living rooms. They are the mentors to the Space Brothers coming in *physical form*. We have stated before that all space beings are not three dimensional. Those operating in space ships above your world that you can see, feel, and touch are the same as you—three dimensional. God's universe is in complete order. The reason you see space ships is because people on other worlds still

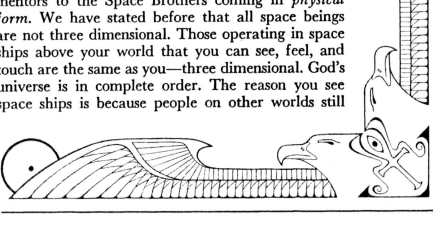

need them and build them in order to travel.

I speak strongly because I feel strongly. I am perturbed at the entire situation that is taking place in the United States of America. I assure you that the New Age work is progressing better in Europe and elsewhere, in Canada, Australia and New Zealand than it is in the United States. What is this statement that the United States will be spared? The United States will be submerged, except for a few mountain places on the east and west coasts. Parts of the four states—Colorado, Utah, Arizona, New Mexico—will remain. But we will not pursue that for the moment. The United States is the centre for the darkest forces upon the Planet Earth.

The United Nations must collapse because that which you read from the Nostradamus forces is true. The war lords, the 'International Bankers' will use the United Nations to form their super-government. This will not be. There are no Christ forces in the United Nations. That does not mean that there are not some good people who are in the United Nations. But the organization itself is a centre, using gullible people. I say it is demon controlled and must go down. The Master has said, and it is written in Corinthians by our beloved Paul: 'All forms of authority and power must be put down before I come.' And the United Nations fits that category.

Everybody wants the New Age, but they want it to be an American New Age, or a British New Age, or a Communistic New Age. I say that *all* forms of government will collapse. Every seat of government will fall utterly and completely. Every economic system will be eliminated. All forms of authority which are under the direct guidance and tutelage of the Black Dragon will perish.

This is an important time. It is the time when the

Anti-Christ himself will appear, but he will be followed as a Master, perhaps even as the return of The Christ. It will not be easy for people to decide between the Christ and Anti-Christ, because both will appear as angels of Light. Both will be beloved of the people. Many of the elect and the select will make the wrong choice. Only the discerning will know.

A false prophet can be determined by the fact that he is the first to throw the stones. Why does a black sheep put on a white sheep's garb, and then dash into the flock of sheep crying, 'Oh, oh! my, my! there's a black sheep somewhere!' It is to draw attention away from himself so that all the sheep are looking at each other because he is afraid his fake sheep's clothing might fall off revealing the wolf.

The next seven years are of great import to the world. We will not relent; we will not say things are getting better all the time. The Bible says, 'When they say peace, watch out!' Things are not getting better but worse. The final thrashing tail of the dying Black Dragon will cause much destruction. Those who say they're working with the Christ forces and are following the messages of the prophets and The Christ, still turn around and say everything is lovely; they do not even believe the prophecies they pretend to believe in.

Is everything lovely in the Bible! Very little is. It is nothing but blood from Genesis to Revelation. The only bright hope in it—all the way through to the coming of the Master—the *only* thing of hope is His message. This is as it should be. The Book of Revelations is anything but a story of a bed of roses, a time of walking in Elysian fields with the Master guiding and leading us to the feast. Yet the conclusion shall be wonderful and beyond belief.

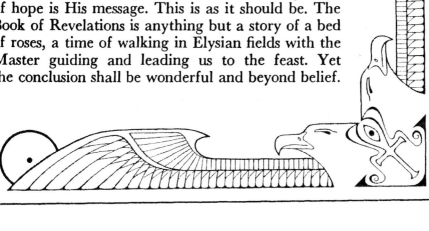

Archangel Michael

Those who think this is the time for hiding will find that their hiding places will fall upon them. Those who say that there will be no destruction, are not aware, nor can they believe in the divine prophecies, both through Jesus the Christ and the holy prophets of all time. If they do not believe that there shall be war in heaven, then they do not believe their own Bibles in Chapter Twelve of the Book of Revelation. If they do not believe that there shall be a judgment upon man and that Jesus the Christ shall come with the holy saints to pronounce this judgment upon the Earth, they do not believe Him! And Jesus the Christ has said: 'Thou art with me or against me.'

These are strong words, but you must believe them. They do not believe the Book of Ezekiel! Or the Book of Isaiah! They do not believe the words of Daniel! They do not believe even Christ when He spoke of the end of the age. And if they do not believe the Book of Revelation then they cannot accept the events now taking place. The Great Deceiver, the serpent, is enticing them to laxity, to go into hiding, to give up the fight! Therefore, warn them! Tell them: 'Dear Christian brethren, take stock of yourselves and reread this Book that you say you believe in. How can you believe part of it and ignore two-thirds of it?'

Let us examine Chapter 12 of Revelation.

Rev. 12:1: And there appeared a great wonder in heaven; a woman clothed with the sun, and the moon under her feet, and upon her head a crown of twelve stars . . .

The woman who is the wonder of our own Solar

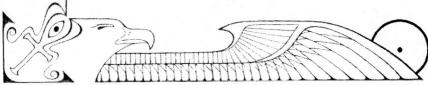

System, not the Earth but the System. The twelve stars in the crown are the twelve planets; the Moon under her feet. Why do they speak of one moon? And clothed with the Sun? The Solar System would be clothed in the Sun, would it not? But why the Moon under her feet? the dark side of night.

It stands for things that are lunar: lunacy; things of the night; secret things.

Rev. 12:2: And she being with child cried, travailing in birth, and pained to be delivered.

Now the Solar System is to be delivered of child. What does this mean? The child is the Earth world. Is not the Solar System travailing in labour for the Earth?

Rev. 12:3: And there appeared another wonder in heaven; and behold a great red dragon, having seven heads and ten horns, and seven crowns upon his heads.

Now here again is the seven and ten. The ten represents the 'Hidden Empire.' The seven was the kings, while the great red dragon symbolizes the negative forces.

Its counterpart upon the Earth, the great beast, also had seven and ten, an exact counterpart of the same force. The great red dragon can also be called the great black dragon, but it is called the great red dragon here.

Rev. 12:4: And his tail drew the third part of the stars of heaven ...

The third part of the stars of heaven is a good number. At the time that this was written about two thousand stars were visible to the naked eye—of course man can still see as many with the naked eye. The third part: 650–700. That is many solar systems, is it not? What could it mean but the third part of the stars of heaven? The tail of the great red dragon

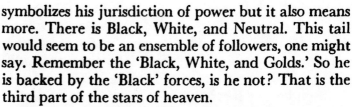

symbolizes his jurisdiction of power but it also means more. There is Black, White, and Neutral. This tail would seem to be an ensemble of followers, one might say. Remember the 'Black, White, and Golds.' So he is backed by the 'Black' forces, is he not? That is the third part of the stars of heaven.

Rev. 12:4: . . . *and did cast them to the earth* . . .

What does that mean? Surely but that they must have incarnated here. And by casting them to the Earth they have now returned; they have begun their campaign in earnest. In other words, this period is now taking place. This chapter is for the present moment.

Rev. 12:4: . . . *and the dragon stood before the woman which was ready to be delivered, for to devour her child as soon as it was born.*

The dragon will devour the child. The Solar System, in other words, is ready to bring its last remaining child into its fold or Tribunal, into the Interplanetary Brotherhood, but the great 'Black' forces will devour this child before it can be placed in this category.

Rev. 12:5: And she brought forth a man child . . .

Is the Earth not always spoken of as Mother Earth? What is this man child situation? The Earth who has been a 'she' is now a 'he.' What does this mean—a man child? It could represent a power or a force. But it also represents the godhood of Earth because those of Earth are destined to rule other planetary systems. You have been told that this is a school for gods—*for* gods, *of* gods, and *by* gods. So, this man child symbolizes this divinity of the Earth children; and it is to be devoured by the great red dragon before it can find its divine mission. But it is caught up.

Rev. 12:5: . . . *who was to rule all nations with a*

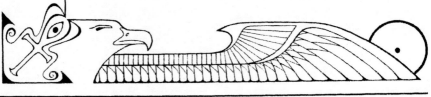

rod of iron . . .

The man child who is to rule all nations, all planetary systems perhaps in this section of the Galaxy, could it be? You will find many times in your Holy Scripture that 'nations' does not refer to earthly kingdoms but refers to other worlds, not always but many times, especially in the prophetic sections. But what is this rod of iron? It does not mean with force, authority or dictatorship; it does not mean that at all.

Rev. 12:5: . . . and her child was caught up unto God, and to his throne.

The child is caught up to God and to the throne. Where is the throne and where is God? On Sirius.

What does this mean, that the Earth will literally be placed upon Sirius? No. But a few children might be caught up.

Rev. 12:6: And the woman fled into the wilderness, where she hath a place prepared of God . . .

The Earth fled into the *wilderness*—the Solar System. Could this not be the magnetic field of the embryonic sun—the *wilderness*?

Rev. 12:6: . . . where she hath a place prepared of God . . .

Yes, indeed, it has been prepared.

Rev. 12:6: . . . that they should feed her there a thousand two hundred and three-score days.

How long is this? It is three and a half years. If we calculate the three and a half years as of now this brings us to 1960—the year of turning perhaps.

Rev. 12:7: And there was war in heaven: Michael and his angels fought against the dragon . . .

Michael and his angels refers to the inhabitants of the worlds beneath the corona of the Sun. What is the nature of the Sun? It is not, of course, cold in the sense of degrees, but it is not a flaming body. What is

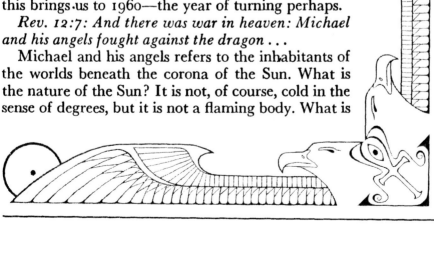

beneath the Solar corona which no man has seen? What do you think is its nature? It is a cool body. What is beneath it? Planets. Everything is duplication in the Father's realm. Study the construction of an atom. There are as many electrons as protons in each. If you have twelve planets without, the Sun is the nucleus; twelve planets are the electrons and within the nucleus are the protons.

Twelve neutrons. What are they—speaking of the System, that is? The twelve bodies beneath the surface of the corona: The Sun is composed of twelve bodies, and their revolutions bring about the strange eleven-year Sun-spot cycle. But the inhabitants—because there are inhabitants upon the Sun—are different from those who inhabit worlds. I could not begin to explain life as it exists there. But they are worlds. Life does not exist in flaming gas. These beings are the angels, so-called. Michael and his legions,—the archangels,—are all sun dwellers.

Why are there only seven archangels? Because there were only seven sacred planets of the ancients. Because they did not have the complete picture this did not mean there were not more. The real ancients knew there were more. Hence the twelve astrological signs, as also the twelve archangels.

Rev. 12:7–8: . . . and the dragon fought and his angels, And prevailed not; neither was their place found any more in heaven.

And now the picture unfolds! The great red dragon did not prevail. What is this war in heaven? Are we going to shoot it out in our space rockets? What kind of war will it be?

It will be a conflict of materialism expressed on the mental plane against spiritual development expressed on the mental plane. It will be a battle of the wits, and it is now raging all about you. Why have we spoken about the Golden Helmeted Ones? The golden helmet does not mean arrayed to keep off arrows or missiles. What is the golden helmet upon the head? What does it mean? Why is this strange helmet found on the ancient Aztec idols? Why is it found throughout Mexico?

Rev. 12:9: And the great dragon was cast out, that old serpent, called the Devil . . .

Here we get to the crux of the matter. The old serpent; the return of the Naga peoples, the Atlans, the Serpent or Snake people, is it not? What does the 'Devil' mean?

Rev. 12:9: And the great dragon was cast out . . .

The great dragon: divided into three separate things, but which has been regarded as being synonymous. The dragon, the 'Devil,' and the serpent have been identified as one. What is the Garden? Is it a small plot of land upon the Earth's surface, or is it the entire creation—this Garden of Eden? Surely the creation.

The dragon is the organization backed by the 'Black' forces. It will be destroyed. The serpent means the race of the Serpent people or the Snake people—the Atlans returning as they promised when they left the Earth, returning to take it.

Now what is 'Devil'? Backwards it spells what '*lived.*' There is no Devil as such. Each man is his own devil, the baser self, the mindless primitive of each man. Devil—*lived*; evil—*live*. Evil backwards is *live*; devil backwards is *lived*. To serve the 'White' forces is to live; to serve the 'Black' is to devil—to die.

Rev. 12:9: . . . and Satan, which deceiveth the whole world . . .

And what is Satan? Spelled backwards it is 'na*t*as,' or 'Nagas.'

Rev. 12:9 . . . he was cast out into the earth, and

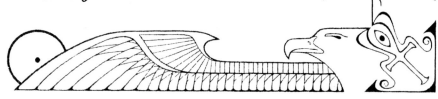

his angels were cast out with him.

This would seem to mean that a certain leader of this group of Serpent people would come with his cohorts. He has already come in the form of Communist Russia, of which Marx and Lenin were chief cohorts.

Rev. 12:10: And I heard a loud voice saying in heaven, Now is come salvation, and strength, and the kingdom of our God . . .

The loud voice from heaven is the proclamation of the Space Confederation backed by the 'White' forces.

Rev. 12:10: . . . and the power of his Christ: for the accuser of our brethren is cast down, which accused them before our God day and night.

Self-explanatory, surely?

Rev. 12:11: And they overcame him by the blood of the Lamb, and by the word of their testimony; and they loved not their lives unto the death.

What is this *blood* of the Lamb? The *life* of the Lamb perhaps.

Rev. 12:12: Therefore rejoice, ye heavens, and ye that dwell in them.

Is this not significant, for this is no reference to an amorphous angelic being? '. . . rejoice, ye heavens, and ye that dwell in them'—a direct statement of other planetary life.

Rev. 12:12–13: Woe to the inhabiters of the earth and of the sea! for the devil is come down unto you, having great wrath, because he knoweth that he hath but a short time. And when the dragon saw that he was cast unto the earth, he persecuted the woman which brought forth the man child.

In the form of your 'Hidden Empire.' This shall be the wrath of the devil upon the surface of the earth.

Rev. 12:14: And to the woman were given two

wings of a great eagle, that she might fly into the wilderness, into her place . . .

How strange! Two wings of a great eagle! What is this that says in the Holy Scripture: you will be caught up! you will meet in the place of the eagles. It refers to spacecraft. Yet this does not mean that the woman, or the Solar System, is going to be taken away. Two wings suggesting flight might imply the achievement of the Theta Universe perhaps. Two wings of an eagle when placed in flight make the letter 'L.'

Rev. 12:14: . . . where she is nourished for a time, and times, and half a time, from the face of the serpent.

Ah! And now the riddle which has always perplexed man! What is this 'time, and times, and half'? 'Time' is a period, and 'times' is plural of that period. Supposing it were a year, times would be two years, half time would be half a year, making a total of three and a half or three dimensions, plus—three dimensions or beyond.

Rev. 12:15: And the serpent cast out of his mouth water as a flood after the woman, that he might cause her to be carried away of the flood.

Not water in the literal sense, naturally. In its different aspects water represents weakness and negativeness, cleansing, mental potentiality and, in some cases, life or vital energy.

Rev. 12:16: And the earth helped the woman, and the earth opened her mouth, and swallowed up the flood which the dragon cast out of his mouth.

How these terms interchange! One minute it is a serpent and the next a dragon; then a devil; then Satan.

Rev. 12:17: And the dragon was wroth with the woman, and went to make war with the remnant of

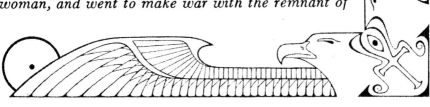

her seed, which keep the commandments of God, and have the testimony of Jesus Christ.

Now it is a dragon again! Each one is used with a particular meaning. One signifies the 'Unholy Six' working with the 'Blacks'; the other the activities of the 'Blacks' upon the Earth, or their representatives, the 'Hidden Empire.' The other term symbolizes the force behind these things. A devil, a dragon—the dragon itself is symbolical and it is always used where they are speaking of the dragon which fights the war in heaven. And it makes war with her seed. What is the 'seed' of the Solar System? What is the 'remnant of the seed' of the Solar System?—It is people, is it not? In other words, we are having a System war. We of this System are being invaded by those of Orion. Therefore the inhabitants of the Sun System, as well as the inhabitants of the outer worlds—twelve in number each—are preparing for that war in heaven, which begins now and continues for the next three and a half years; which also corresponds to the three and a half of the 'time, and times, and half.'

Master Kuthumi

The first part of this message is directed to those who serve in the Light. Before long a purge may come to some of you who serve in the Light. But take no heed. And, should it do so, I want you to use as a reference and proof a certain scripture from the Gospel of St. Mark.

St. Mark 13:9–20: But take heed to yourselves: for they shall deliver you up to councils; and in the synagogues ye shall be beaten: and ye shall be brought before rulers and kings for my sake, for a

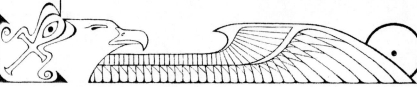

testimony against them. And the gospel must first be published among all nations. But when they shall lead you, *and deliver you up, take no thought beforehand what ye shall speak, neither do ye premeditate: but whatsoever shall be given you in that hour, that speak ye: for it is not ye that speak, but the Holy Ghost. Now the brother shall betray the brother to death, and the father the son; and children shall rise up against* their *parents, and shall cause them to be put to death. And ye shall be hated of all* men *for my name's sake: but he that shall endure unto the end, the same shall be saved. But when ye shall see the abomination of desolation, spoken of by Daniel the prophet, standing where it ought not (let him that readeth understand), then let them that be in Judaea flee to the mountains: And let him that is on the housetop not go down into the house, neither enter* therein, *to take any thing out of his house: And let him that is in the field not turn back again for to take up his garment. But woe to them that are with child, and to them that give suck in those days! And pray ye that your flight be not in the winter. For* in *those days shall be affliction, such as was not from the beginning of the creation which God created unto this time, neither shall be. And except that the Lord had shortened those days, no flesh should be saved: but for the elect's sake, whom he hath chosen, he hath shortened the days.*

They say there is no chance of such a thing. They also say there will be no wars, no catastrophe. All is peace; all is love. But what of the message in Christ's own words as recorded by Mark. They are true words, for Mark heard them himself. Because they *will* deliver you up.

Rev. 3:14–16: And unto the angel of the church of the Laodiceans write; These things saith the

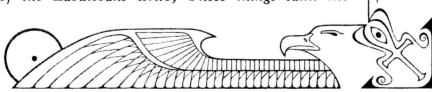

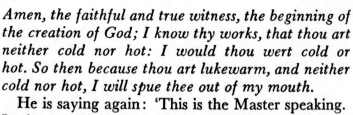

Amen, the faithful and true witness, the beginning of the creation of God; I know thy works, that thou art neither cold nor hot: I would thou wert cold or hot. So then because thou art lukewarm, and neither cold nor hot, I will spue thee out of my mouth.

He is saying again: 'This is the Master speaking. In the new Bible version it says, 'I will vomit you up.' He would rather have you completely indifferent to His word than lukewarm because you know the truth and yet you exercise it not. Were that you were cold, ignorant of the facts! 'I would rather have you cold or hot but not *lukewarm.*' Lukewarm Christians will be spewed out of the mouth of the Elder Brother and the Father.

Tell them: where is your faith? If you do not believe in the promises that He has given. If we are His children, yea even His sons, will He not be with us? Lukewarm Christians beware!

Rev. 3:17: Because thou sayest, I am rich, and increased with goods, and have need of nothing; and knowest not that thou art wretched, and miserable, and poor, and blind, and naked ...

'Yes, I am a good Christian. I go to church every Sunday. I haven't missed a Sunday in twenty-five years. You see that panel in the church window over there—that new frosted glass panel—I donated that to the church. It cost £100. I give to the missionary funds, to the building funds, to the hospital funds, to the orphan fund. I am rich; I have plenty. I am a Christian, but I don't believe the promises of God. I don't even believe in eternal life. I doubt it at times; in fact, I doubt it quite often. I don't like to think of death because really I don't believe in eternal life. I worry about my illnesses and about my troubles, but I don't take them to the Father who has promised He

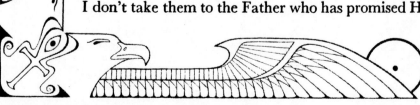

will do all and take care of all. I don't have the faith.'
How often we hear this from 'good' Christians!

*Rev. 3:18–22: I counsel thee to buy of me gold
tried in the fire, that thou mayest be rich; and white
raiment, that thou mayest be clothed, and that the
shame of thy nakedness do not appear; and anoint
thine eyes with eyesalve, that thou mayest see. As
many as I love, I rebuke and chasten: be zealous
therefore, and repent. Behold, I stand at the door,
and knock: if any man hear my voice, and open the
door, I will come in to him, and will sup with him,
and he with me. To him that overcometh will I grant
to sit with me in my throne, even as I also overcame,
and am set down with my Father in his throne. He
that hath an ear, let him hear what the Spirit saith
unto the churches.*

Yes, he that has an ear! Tell your people that this
is the message: he that hath an ear, let him listen.
Lukewarm Buddhist, lukewarm Moslem, lukewarm
Christian: the Master stands at the door and knocks!
It is time that we forgot our lukewarmness. Be either
cold or hot, but choose one or the other!

This is the time of 'revolution'! It is the time for
those who are pure of heart to rise up and put down
the dark forces of the Earth. This is not a time for
'lollygagging' in churches, nor a time to be moving in
secular societies, worried in church over the Ladies'
Aid. Get on fire, Christians! because the negative
'Black' forces are deluding you! *Wake up* or you will
be vomited from the Master's mouth.

Once again I am on my fiery tour. It amuses me
that people cannot accept this as Master K. H. because I am supposed to be a silly monk sitting by the
roadside on his bed of nails contemplating the Sun.
They believe that periodically from out of Shigatse
I should make some such statement as: 'Within the

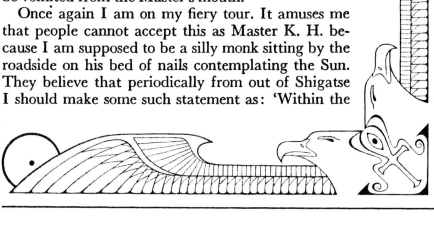

thousand petalled lotus dwells all wisdom: God is love; God is peace.' No! This is a time for men and masters of *action* and not a time for meditation.

This is the time of the end of which Christ spoke. He was a man of action! When He stood before the tomb of Lazarus He cried, 'Come forth! I command! In the name of the Father!' Lukewarmness is *not* of the Father. Be strong! *Know* wherein ye speak and wherein ye stand, and know the true Church of Christ, which is His Mystical Body.

If, at any time, you are delivered up in this life or in a million lifetimes hence, think not what you will say. But if you must speak outside of the Father and of your own volition, say that you have a mission on the Earth, that you have deceived no one, no country, no thing. You are only serving the true Creator. Tell them you are answerable to no one for your actions but Him. And they will reply: 'Carry him away and crucify him,' even as they did the Master, 'for speaking such blasphemy,' and for calling yourself a son of God. Yet the poor fools do not know that they, too, are sons of God.

Master Hilarion

Let us study certain portions of the Bible.

I Corinthians 12:1–31: Now concerning spiritual gifts, brethren, I would not have you ignorant. Ye know that ye were Gentiles, carried away unto these dumb idols, even as ye were led. Wherefore I give you to understand, that no man speaking by the Spirit of God calleth Jesus accursed: and that no man can say that Jesus is the Lord, but by the Holy Ghost. Now there are diversities of gifts, but the same

Spirit. And there are differences of administrations, but the same Lord, And there are diversities of operations, but it is the same God which worketh all in all. But the manifestation of the Spirit is given to every man to profit withal. For to one is given by the Spirit the word of wisdom; to another the word of knowledge by the same Spirit; To another faith by the same Spirit; to another the gifts of healing by the same Spirit; To another the working of miracles; to another prophecy: to another discerning of spirits; to another divers kinds of tongues; to another the interpretation of tongues: But all these worketh that one and the selfsame Spirit, dividing to every man severally as he will. For as the body is one, and hath many members, and all the members of that one body, being many, are one body: so also is Christ. For by one Spirit are we all baptized into one body, whether we be Jews or Gentiles, whether we be bond or free; and have been all made to drink into one Spirit. For the body is not one member, but many. If the foot shall say, Because I am not the hand, I am not of the body; is it therefore not of the body? And if the ear shall say, Because I am not the eye, I am not of the body; is it therefore not of the body? If the whole body were an eye, where were the hearing? If the whole were hearing, where were the smelling? But now hath God set the members every one of them in the body, as it hath pleased him. And if they were all one member, where were the body? But now are they many members, yet but one body. And the eye cannot say unto the hand, I have no need of thee: nor again the head to the feet, I have no need of you. Nay, much more those members of the body, which seem to be more feeble, are necessary: And those members of the body, which we think to be less honourable, upon these we bestow more abundant

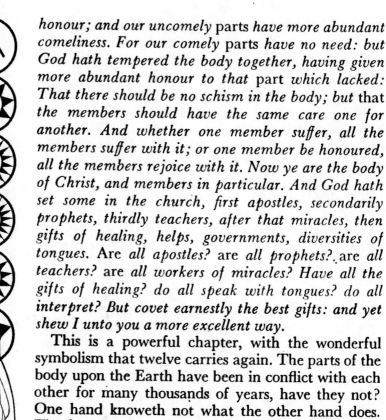

honour; and our uncomely parts have more abundant comeliness. For our comely parts have no need: but God hath tempered the body together, having given more abundant honour to that part which lacked: That there should be no schism in the body; but that the members should have the same care one for another. And whether one member suffer, all the members suffer with it; or one member be honoured, all the members rejoice with it. Now ye are the body of Christ, and members in particular. And God hath set some in the church, first apostles, secondarily prophets, thirdly teachers, after that miracles, then gifts of healing, helps, governments, diversities of tongues. Are all apostles? are all prophets?, are all teachers? are all workers of miracles? Have all the gifts of healing? do all speak with tongues? do all interpret? But covet earnestly the best gifts: and yet shew I unto you a more excellent way.

This is a powerful chapter, with the wonderful symbolism that twelve carries again. The parts of the body upon the Earth have been in conflict with each other for many thousands of years, have they not? One hand knoweth not what the other hand does. The feet go where the head directs not. They are in conflict. And when we speak of the one body in Christ we speak of all His children and the sheep of His flock upon the Planet Earth.

But the times are changing and there will no longer be that conflict. We are being brought to perfection into one body in the Christ vibration. If each part is not in harmony with the other, is out of cosmic rhythm, then there is discord and conflict, and this is the basis for individual 'dis-ease.'

This chapter speaks of gifts of the Spirit from our Infinite Father. Some shall speak with tongues: *Isha malai tai tou.* Some shall interpret the tongues. 'From

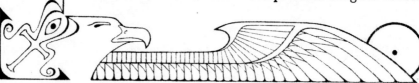

the Eternal Flame,' I said, 'comes all wisdom.' So there shall be tongues spoken and those to translate tongues. There shall be prophets and apostles. There shall be wisdom and knowledge. Wisdom is not knowledge nor is knowledge wisdom. You do not attain wisdom merely because you have knowledge.

I take my next quotation from Malachi, the last chapter, and the last Book of the Old Testament.

Malachi 4:1–6: For, behold, the day cometh, that shall burn as an oven; and all the proud, yea, and all that do wickedly, shall be stubble: and the day that cometh shall burn them up, saith the Lord of hosts, that it shall leave them neither root nor branch. But unto you that fear my name shall the Sun of righteousness arise with healing in his wings; and ye shall go forth, and grow up as calves of the stall. And ye shall tread down the wicked; for they shall be ashes under the soles of your feet in the day that I shall do this, saith the Lord of hosts. Remember ye the law of Moses my servant, which I command unto him in Horeb for all Israel, with the statutes and judgments. *Behold, I will send you Elijah the prophet before the coming of the great and dreadful day of the Lord: And he shall turn the heart of the fathers to the children, and the heart of the children to their fathers, lest I come and smite the earth with a curse.*

Is this not a beautiful chapter?—Elijah comes before the great and terrible day of the Lord. John the Baptist comes. Is it not written thusly? Now read again of the Sun of righteousness, for it is an important verse.

Malachi 4:2: But unto you that fear my name shall the Sun of righteousness arise with healing in his wings . . .

Our message is directed to the *Remnant,* to no other. After the time of tribulation and the establish-

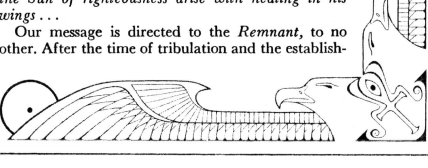

ment of the Millennium upon the Earth, some say, 'How will I fit into this period with my Lord? I have no legs; I am in the last stages of cancer.' We speak of those negative, physical conditions, but the people of the world want to know and they have a right to know the answer.

The Sun of righteousness shall arise with healing in His wings! Therefore, at His Second Coming there shall be Divine healing throughout the Remnant that remains. It speaks of the day that shall be like an oven, of those who will be removed from the Earth and burned like stubble; and the Remnant shall walk upon the stubble and the ashes shall be ground beneath their feet. And those who would enslave man physically, mentally, and spiritually, will go back to the dust from whence they came; and their souls shall go elsewhere for a new expression, for a new cycle, verily. But remember, The Sun of righteousness arises with healing in His wings! It is even now coming.

Proverbs 3:8: It shall be health to thy navel, and marrow to thy bones.

What is this strange verse? What, in the name of all that is holy, is health to your navel or medicine to your navel—it can also be translated as 'medicine.' The navel is the region of the solar plexus. And what is the solar plexus? It's sort of an abdominal brain. It is also the centre of a chakra. This is one of the most vital areas, because we have so much emotional upset and conditions in the world today. Above all others it is influenced greatly by mental conditions. Mental tension today is the cause of ulcers and gall-bladder troubles. It is not in balance. A great vortex exists at this point, this chakra, bringing in many beneficial vibrations or rays from without. Now it shall be health, or like medicine, to thy *navel* or solar plexus and as marrow to the bones.

What is this new vibration which the Earth is now entering into, this new dimension of Time and Space? Its effects will be felt mainly through the solar plexus. But it does not come until His Second Coming. Then the healing in His wings: it is health to thy solar plexus. This new condition can do naught else but heal, cleanse and purify those who remain. This shall be their inheritance: perfect health and the elimination of all disease. For once He arises into His kingdom and takes those who are His unto Himself, this vibration will do its own work.

St. Mark 16:17–18: And these signs shall follow them that believe; In my name shall they cast out devils; they shall speak with new tongues; They shall take up serpents; and if they drink any deadly thing, it shall not hurt them; they shall lay hands on the sick, and they shall recover.

What is meant here in the reference to serpents? It is a promise. The Bible is full of the promise of God. This is a promise written in Mark that they *shall* take up serpents and they *will* drink any deadly or poisonous thing and it will *not* hurt them. Now, tell your people that I say this: They go to church on Sunday and they believe in life after death on Sunday, and in divine healing and miracles on Sunday; they believe in the Christ who walked upon the waters and healed the sick and raised the dead and who Himself was resurrected from the dead. They believe this on Sunday, but the rest of the week they remove this cloak of belief and have great fear and do not believe, and their faith is small. For this is a promise of God: we believe or we do not believe it. God is speaking Truth or God is a liar! He has promised us that we can take up serpents and can drink any deadly thing and it will not hurt us. So be it.

But *we are not to tempt God!* If we happen upon

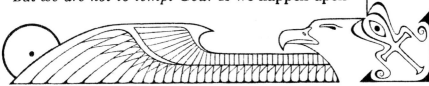

a snake or by chance drink poison from those who would destroy us, we *will* be protected. But do not tempt the Father.

St. Luke 10:19: Behold, I give unto you power to tread on serpents and scorpions, and over all the power of the enemy: and nothing shall by any means hurt you.

Again, the Father's promise! We can tread upon serpents and scorpions. He gives us that power. And His further promise of power over the enemy—the enemy which is the anti-Christ, which we recognize in the International Bankers and the others who would enslave man upon the Earth, the negative 'Black' forces. God says I will give you power over *all.*

Finally, nothing by any means shall hurt you. *No thing!* This promise is overlooked by the Fundamentalists and by others who deny Divine Healing and other so-called miracles of the Infinite Father. God promises to the Remnant that will remain—not to the 'Black' forces but to His own children—that *nothing* at all will hurt them. Why then do they fear? Why do they cringe from Monday to Saturday and on Sunday believe?

Rev. 22:2: In the midst of the street of it, and on either side of the river, was there the tree of life, which bare twelve manner of fruits, and yielded her fruit every month: and the leaves of the tree were for the healing of the nations.

What is this tree? More important than the healing of an individual man is the healing of the nations, and not only the nations of the Earth are meant here. 'Nations' mean, in Michael's words, other worlds— the healing of the twelve in this System, bringing back the wayward Earth into the Interplanetry Tribunal, the Interplanetary Brotherhood.

When we speak of health and healing not only do we speak of individual man with his gout and his toothaches and his cancer, we speak of the nations that are also cancerous, diseased, degenerate, and dying. So therefore it is a promise of God in the last book of Holy Scriptures that the nations shall be healed when it speaks of 'the leaves thereof for the healing of the nations.'

Now what are the twelve fruits? Every month the fruits are given. The fruits are the gifts of the Spirit that shall be given to the nations, and the leaves thereof for their healing. This shall heal the nations of Earth and bring them together in the one great body in which the members will not be in conflict with each other. One foot will not say, 'I shall go west'; the other, 'I shall go east.' The body shall be *one* because the nations shall be healed. It shall be one world, not under the United Nations, but under Christ the King, Lord of the Earth.

St. Luke 4:22: And all bare him witness, and wondered at the gracious words which proceeded out of his mouth. And they said, Is not this Joseph's son? And he said unto them, Ye will surely say unto me this proverb, Physician, heal thyself; whatsoever we have heard done in Capernaum, do also here in thy country. And he said, Verily I say unto you, No prophet is accepted in his own country.

There are two points here of importance: One, 'Physician heal thyself,' which the people of Nazareth, who rejected the Christ, said to Jesus. And the second point is, a prophet is never accepted in his own country! The people said, 'Physician, if you are so great and what you claim to be, heal thyself.' Now, there shall be those scoffers and mockers in the days immediately ahead who will say to those working with the Mystery Schools, 'If you have this thing,

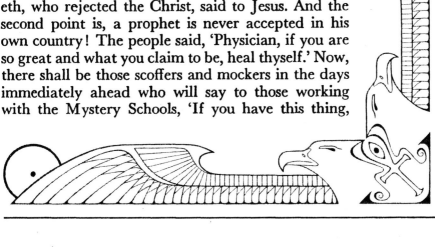

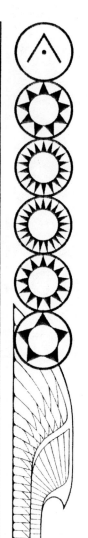

heal thyself.' For many of you are not completely fit. Perhaps this unfit condition is for the fulfilment of the word and perhaps you were born so that this work may be shown, even as the man who was healed by the Master. The Master said his condition was not due to the sins of the mother or father, or even his own sins, but so that he might be an example. Therefore, when they say 'Heal thyself,' the Remnant shall demonstrate and shall heal themselves, for it is up to each man to perfect himself through Christ.

Lord Aramu-Muru (God Meru)

Love, light, and peace to all those who feel that they are in body, heart, and soul part of the Brotherhood of the Seven Rays. To all those wherever they might be who feel that they are part of Christ's Kingdom upon the Earth, shortly to reveal itself.

Never before in the history of the Mystery Schools of Earth has one in my position been called upon or, indeed, been given the authority to extend an open invitation to all those who would take up their cross and follow the Master, an invitation for them to come and join in the work of the Mystery School known as the Brotherhood of the Seven Rays.

Shortly come the drums of war—twin to the brother drum of death and destruction—when the four horsemen ride wild the night wind upon the Earth.

Rev. 18:4: And I heard another voice from heaven, saying, Come out of her, my people, that ye be not partakers of her sins, and that ye receive not of her plagues.

Rev. 22:10–17: And he saith unto me, Seal not the sayings of the prophecy of this book: for the time is at hand. He that is unjust, let him be unjust still: and he which is filthy, let him be filthy still: and he that is righteous, let him be righteous still: and he that is holy, let him be holy still. And, behold, I come quickly; and my reward is with me, to give every man according as his work shall be. I am Alpha and Omega, the beginning and the end, the first and the last. Blessed are they that do his commandments, that they may have right to the tree of life, and may enter in through the gates into the city. For without are dogs, and sorcerers, and whoremongers, and murderers, and idolators, and whosoever loveth and maketh a lie. I Jesus have sent mine angel to testify unto you these things in the churches. I am the root and the offspring of David, and the bright and morning star. And the Spirit and the bride say, Come. And let him that heareth say, Come. And let him that is athirst come. And whosoever will, let him take the water of life freely.

Rev. 22:17: And the Spirit and the bride say, Come.

This pertains to 'Come out, my people.' The Spirit and the bride say, 'Come.'

Rev. 22:17: And let him that heareth say, Come.

And he that hears. In other words, he that hears and understands will lead and say, 'Come.'

Rev. 22:17: And let him that is athirst come.

He that is hungry and thirsty for spiritual knowledge, he, too, is invited. Come out of her, my people: the abominable Babylon—not referring here to any nation but 'Babylon,' meaning the materialism of the world. This is an open invitation to all those who would align themselves with Right, and Good, and Truth, and Light, and Peace, and Brotherhood.

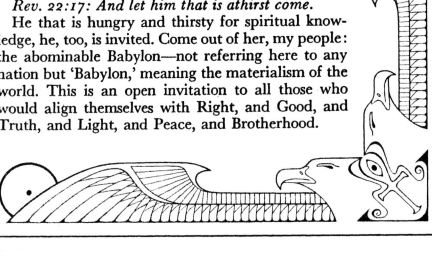

We of the Brotherhood of the Seven Rays, having established for the first time in metaphysical history a centre outside of our own monastery at Lake Titicaca, invite those students of Light of any age, sex, race, creed, colour, or ideology, to join us. But yea, only those who *belong* will find their way to the gate of the Abbey. Only those who belong will come for, even if they leave the next day, it was necessary that they come.

Upon the horizon Armageddon is shortly to come to pass. The forces of darkness are aligning themselves for the final death throes of darkness upon the Earth. We can hear the marching feet, for they are now—even now—marching upon the etheric planes, shortly to find physical manifestation upon the Earth. But the great army will be swallowed up in cataclysm as the islands move out of their place upon the face of the Earth, as it is written; and as fire —literal fire—rains down from the heavens, and the angel casts the great stone into the ocean as a sign to all nations and peoples.

We say, 'Come out, our people': you who have seen the handwriting, even as Daniel, as it stands out in fire from the wall of the present time; you who know in your hearts that this is the time of the coming of our Elder Brother; you who know that the Elder Brother shall shortly speak unto thee: *Come out!* come out!

We ask, as our blessed Elder Brother asked the rich young ruler who was so intent on serving, to give up all: your 'crown,' your 'jewels,' your 'treasures' stored on the face of the Earth.

But, yet, this is their test of faith for, as Abbot of the Monastery of the Brotherhood of the Seven Rays, I guarantee—speaking in the Light of the Father—that the most astounding revelations of a spiritual nature shall be theirs if they forsake all, even as you are forsaking all for this work. Yet in forsaking all you shall find vast 'treasure' of which you have never dreamed. In the lands of Brazil in particular and even in our own country of Peru, you and they will stand within the limits of literal tons of gold and jewels, the accumulated riches of the Earth buried for centuries and some for thousands of years: jewels and treasures to stagger the mind of man. But we are not offering jewels to those who give up and forsake all. The jewels will mean nothing to them. This is God's strange paradox: Give up *all* and you shall find yourselves amongst the greatest treasure the world has ever known or seen; but then it will mean nothing to you, and you will not covet, nor will you desire it for your own.

He who will exalt himself will be humbled. Humble thyself and you shall be exalted. Be a king and you shall be a slave, but be a slave and you shall be a king.

We say now, listen to the still small voice within. Come out and make a sign! If you believe these things you have been told, then make a sign that you believe. We cannot have spirituality of a celestial nature and yet partake of the flesh of the physical world. Let us follow in the footsteps of Him—the one whom we all know as our Elder Brother—He who was meek, lowly and humble.

Our command to all of you who read and understand and love and know this message of Light and Truth and Peace, a Divine command from the Father is this: Make ready for the prepared people, for thy Elder Brother will shortly speak unto thee.

God the Father has promised: 'I will bring them to My holy mount. Yea, verily, I shall bring them in Truth and Peace and Light to My holy mountain.'

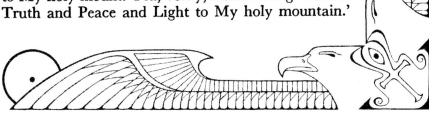

Come Out, My People. Come out with joy! Go forth with peace.

Many will not respond to this message for they are wrapped in materialism, even though they read these messages and feign an interest in matters spiritual. But the time is at hand when those who truly believe must make a sign and follow Him who is the Way, the Truth, and the Life. If He is the *Way* we need no other; if He is the *Truth* and the *Life* we need not turn elsewhere to find it. He who sacrifices his life shall truly find it; he who sacrifices the life of the world will find the life eternal.

Publisher's Note:

By using the term "come out and make a sign," it is not meant for individuals to write personally to Brother Philip or to the Monastery. If exact directions were to be given, they would have appeared in this book. This is a spiritual quest! The book makes it clear that those seeking will find all answers within. If specific instructions are not received by the sincere student, they should not contemplate any journey to Peru and the Andes. Writing letters will accomplish nothing. Also, there is a group in Spain and others elsewhere in the world who are using and capitalizing on the name of the Brotherhood of the Seven Rays. However, none of them have any connection whatsoever with the ancient and original Brotherhood of the Seven Rays refered to in this book. Any group that advertises and sells its "secrets" could never possibly be affiliated with the true Brotherhood. Students must be aware of this fact and act accordingly.

October, 1979

Printed in the United States
713800003B